PREPARING FOR PLATFORM AND PULPIT

John E. Baird

PREPARING FOR PLATFORM AND PULPIT

Abingdon Press

NASHVILLE

NEW YORK

PREPARING FOR PLATFORM AND PULPIT

Copyright © 1968 by Abingdon Press

Library of Congress Catalog Card Number: 68-11468

SET UP, PRINTED, AND BOUND BY THE
PARTHENON   PRESS,   AT   NASHVILLE,
TENNESSEE, UNITED STATES OF AMERICA

To
Roy C. McCall

*Who furnished both the knowledge
and the inspiration
for these pages*

FOREWORD

This book is primarily intended for the minister and is designed to help him prepare for one of his most important functions, the preparation and delivery of Sunday's sermon. It is not intended as a substitute for any of the fine discussions of preaching which are available. Rather, this work is focused on the more general area of public speaking. Its particular aim is to supply the basic skills and understandings required of the man who would preach, those concepts which most of the books in the field of homiletics assume to be familiar to their readers. This text should be of help to undergraduates who plan to prepare for the ministry, to seminarians getting ready for their work in homiletics, to those who are beginning the classroom study of preaching and who need a review of speech organization, to laymen who wish to be more effective on those occasions when they address the congregation, and to ordained ministers who desire to renew their understanding of the basic principles of public speaking.

This book does not subscribe to the philosophy that preaching

is some peculiar or extraordinary application of mysterious principles of occult communication. On the contrary, homiletics is
viewed here as a more limited application of the knowledge and
skill common to all public speaking. Some would deny that any
study of preaching is necessary or proper; the Holy Spirit is said
to inspire his spokesmen when they confront an audience. Even
then, however, the speakers who have best developed their talents
have the most to offer for their divine calling. Insofar as preaching involves those basic understandings and skills common to
all communicative acts, this book should help to make the
preacher more effective.

These pages do not concentrate on voice and diction, although
the aspects of the speaker's delivery will receive attention at the
appropriate time. Speech content and delivery must be regarded
as two aspects of the same thing. Thought cannot be separated
from the words which embody it; neither can those words be
separated from the manner in which they are pronounced. The
principles of content and delivery may fall under separate headings for purposes of analysis, but the teacher must ultimately
synthesize them into the total speech personality of the student.
This text tries to assist the teacher in that process by centering
on the total act of public speaking and attempting to relate the
discussion of each part back to the whole.

Learning to speak effectively involves far more than picking
up a few simple tricks of the trade. The assignments in this book
concentrate upon understanding as well as upon skill. They do
not ask the student to write or to speak on the basis of intensive
research into some area of human knowledge, for such study will
come later in the years which will be spent in the seminary classroom and the church study. Rather, this text emphasizes speaking from experience in the hope that the student will become
proficient in the direct, personal witness which is one vital element in all true preaching. Such speaking does not require excessive amounts of time for preparation. The student is encouraged to spend the bulk of his available time in reading and

writing on rhetorical theory in the hope that his understanding will be deepened, his historical perspective increased, and his skill in handling the language improved.

While this book may be used by anyone wanting to study the principles of public discourse in a logical and orderly fashion, it is primarily planned for use in the classroom. It partakes of many of the characteristics of the so-called "teaching machine," of programmed learning, in that it introduces theory in logical order, one step at a time, each unit building on the units before it. The various assignments which are to be carried out, both within and outside the classroom, are designed to stimulate the active participation of the student in the learning process and are directly related to the work of each unit. While some experienced teachers may wish to substitute their own favorite assignments for those given, students and teacher alike should regard all assignments as inherent parts of the unit, not as a collection of "busy work" appended to each chapter.

The order in which material is presented in these pages has been carefully planned. Students should be warned not to read ahead; teachers will want to think carefully before assigning chapters in any other order. The topic of stage fright is one important case in point. The student will find no mention of this subject in the early pages of this book. He is to focus his attention upon the message which he has to convey and to avoid an unhealthy introspection of his own emotional states. The thoughtless introduction of this topic at the beginning of a public speaking course, a mistake made by many outstanding textbooks, could easily multiply the student's fears, particularly if he lacks an experienced teacher to reassure him.

The evaluation of the student's work, whether in terms of critique or of the grade assigned, should also follow the order in which material is presented in these pages. The student is only responsible for that body of theory which has been assigned to him. He should not be penalized for shortcomings in areas which have not yet been discussed; neither should he receive undue credit if he happens to display an accidental skill in those areas.

Ministers in service who wish to use this text for preaching improvement outside the classroom should begin with the speaking assignment for the second chapter. A series of nine sermons, each planned to meet the requirements of each succeeding chapter and evaluated in those terms, should contribute as much to an individual's development as a speaker as he can expect to gain without the services of an expert teacher.

If this text is successful in the accomplishment of its various objectives, primary credit should go to Dr. Roy C. McCall, whose influence will be found on almost every page and to whom the volume is dedicated, and to hundreds of long-suffering students whose failures and successes taught the writer what little he knows about teaching.

JOHN E. BAIRD

CONTENTS

1

Your Introduction to Speech

BASIC IDEAS

You are about to begin a course of instruction. For some of
you, this occasion marks your first experience with a "speech"
course. Others may have had a great deal of background in oral
expression. You may have had extensive experience as a preacher
or Sunday school teacher. Perhaps you have acted in a school or
community theater, served on a church committee, or held office
in a social or civic organization. You may have had a formal
course in public speaking, homiletics, or oral communication, or
your speech experience may be limited to dinner table conversation. No matter what your background, your feelings about taking this course or even reading this text probably depend upon
your memories of this previous experience. Some of these will
probably be pleasant, others painful. The following considerations should help you understand your own feelings and should
better prepare you for the study that lies ahead.

Speech is a social activity. A castaway on a desert island would have little or no need for speech. Man began to talk in a social environment, as he became aware of his fellows. A person who talks to himself for the sake of hearing himself is often considered a fit subject for confinement in an institution. Speaking to an audience must involve communication with the individuals who compose that audience. The platform or pulpit speaker is never just putting on a show to attract attention; he is exchanging ideas with his listeners.

The process of speaking should be a real exchange of ideas, not merely the verbal expression of the thoughts of the speaker. Communication is a circular process by which thoughts are coded into language, language is transmitted to a hearer, corresponding thoughts are created in the listener's mind, and a response is generated, expressed, and finally perceived by the original speaker. Thus effective public speaking involves listening with ear and eye, even while a speaker is talking to the people before him. Many speakers have failed because they ignored this principle and made their speech an instrument of display rather than of communication.

On the other hand, those who are able to communicate enjoy tremendous social advantages. Talk effectively, and you can translate your personal ideas of Christian stewardship into the most successful budget-raising campaign your church has ever had. You can make your suggestion at a business meeting into a program of action for the entire organization. You can transform your ideas about a candidate into enough votes to put him into office. Words are deeds that can change lives, and such deeds have even changed history. Thus the early Christians gave voice to a gospel which many thinkers of their day considered "foolishness," and their preaching proved to be the very power of God to those who were being saved. They embodied their message in words and deeds and enlisted the popular support to revolutionize a pagan empire. Speak well, and you may exercise a tremendous influence on human society. Always be sure to use that power wisely.

Speech develops the personality. Psychologists generally agree that speech and personality are very closely associated. Think of some of the people you know. Isn't your opinion of their personalities determined to some extent by their speech? If you hear a man talk to a child or a dog, you can form some judgment as to his liking for animals or children. Add further observations, and you begin to form some idea of the person he really is. Even the manner in which he speaks is important. If a man speaks in a big, hearty bass voice, you probably decide that he's the friendly sort you would like to meet. On the other hand, if he talks in a thin, weak tenor, you probably decide that he's a henpecked soul who is dominated by his wife!

Other people form judgments of you in exactly the same way. If your speech is indecisive or confused, your associates probably think your mind is equally confused. If your voice is thin and weak, your neighbors probably think you lack backbone. To change these opinions, change your speech! If you speak in a logical, decisive manner, you'll be known as a clear thinker. If your voice is strong and emphatic, you'll be known as a person of determination. If you can address any group with something of significance to say, you will get credit for leadership ability. Furthermore, these reactions to your personality will also be associated with the significance of the message which you have to convey. The most crucial issue can seem trivial if it is discussed in a weak, ineffective manner.

Some may object that changes in speech habits would constitute a gigantic fraud, a form of hypocrisy, a pretending to be something you are not. They think of improved speech habits as a woman might think of cosmetics, as something spread on the surface to hide the blemishes. Perhaps you feel that your own speech habits leave much to be desired, but you would rather fail at being yourself than succeed by pretending to be someone else.

Such views ignore the close interrelationship between speech and personality. Improvements made in your speech habits will not be merely a false front worn in public. As you learn to organize ideas for a speech, you will develop habits of thought that will apply to every problem. The determination that you exhibit from the platform will become characteristic of your attack upon any difficult situation. In other words, changes made in the way you speak tend to become a genuine part of what you really are. These improvements are not cosmetics painted on the surface. Rather, they are like some happy secret which, once you know it, inevitably shows in the expression on your face and influences all of your relationships.

What we are saying is that speech improvement, as we shall attempt to achieve it, comes as a result of changes in the total personality. The avenue that we shall use to effect these changes, however, involves understanding and directed experience in the complex social situation which communicating entails. You must do much more than just learn facts about the theory of public speaking, important as those facts may be. You must not be content with the achievement of clear articulation and graceful gestures; the old courses in elocution failed to produce those basic changes which effective speaking demands. You are to become the intelligent, dynamic, persuasive personality who can adequately represent the force of the ideas he is seeking to communicate. Just as you are now, in part, the product of your past experiences, so you shall be changed by the experiences which lie ahead of you in this course of study.

Speech is an intellectual discipline. Communication traditionally includes five subareas. These are speaking and listening, writing and reading, and critical thinking. Of these five, the last is basic and the most important. Speaking is not just a process of filling the air with verbal symbols. The good speaker conveys significant ideas with force and intelligence. He has learned when to keep still as well as when to talk. The rule is: "Stand up to be seen; speak up to be heard; shut up to be appreciated." The speaker with nothing to say would be better off saying nothing. Speech must be preceded and accompanied by thought. Fail to think first, and you may be sorry you ever spoke.

A solid background of information and ideas is essential for the content of a speech, but the need for careful thinking is not limited to this one area. The person who would speak well must also clearly understand the communicative process which he is using. He must, as one ancient philosopher put it, understand the souls of the men to whom he speaks. In modern terms, the more you can learn about psychology, sociology, and anthropology, the more effective you will be as a speaker. The ideal student of public speaking should learn the physical processes by which he produces the sounds of his language, the physical principles involved in the transmission of those sounds through the atmosphere, and the operation of the ear which receives the sound. He should know something of semantics, the study of meanings. Let him also become acquainted with the language in which he will speak, enriching his vocabulary and learning something of the history and characteristics of English. Acoustics is another important study because of the places in which he may be called upon to speak, and the study of electronics is important because his speaking may involve the use of radio, television, or a public-address system. The list is almost endless. Above all, the skilled speaker should be acquainted with the long history of rhetoric (as public speaking used to be called) so that he may appreciate how its principles have developed and changed, or failed to change, over the years. Is it any wonder that in ancient times the study of rhetoric was the very heart of the entire process of education?

Such an ideal speaker has probably never existed in real life. Nevertheless, the ideal stands in judgment upon each of us with our limited backgrounds and capabilities. Perhaps you picked up this book with the thought of acquiring a few simple techniques which would, overnight, transform you into a great orator. After all, you thought, anyone can talk, and public speaking is only talking a bit more loudly. Just learn a few little skills and rules, get a lot of practice, and go out prepared to persuade lions to become vegetarians.

If these were your thoughts, the rest of this book will disappoint and discourage you. The glib talk that sounds so smooth but says nothing will receive little credit. You will be asked to read what many others have written about the broad field of rhetoric. You will be encouraged to write in order that your style—the way in which you express yourself in words—may be polished through practice and analysis. Each speech that you give will be expected to conform to a clear, specific assignment designed to make you more effective in some phase of public address. You will be asked to listen critically to other speakers, becoming aware of their strengths and weaknesses in order to improve your own speaking. All of these things are important because speech is an intellectual discipline. You should learn to speak well, not by chance or merely by habit, but because you know what you are doing and why you are doing it.

The importance of proper planning for each speech that you give cannot be overemphasized. We must admit that some speeches seem highly successful by pure chance. Some speakers may be very effective at moving an audience by instinct rather than by knowledge; they speak well with no true understanding of their art. However, the speech that succeeds by chance can just as easily fail by chance. Our major concern is with speech improvement, and increased understanding of any art should lead to improved performance in that art. Let each speaker carefully analyze all possible factors in regard to the occasion of speaking, the audience, and the speech itself before he ever rises to deliver that speech. Then if he succeeds, he will know the reasons for his success. If he fails, he will be able to discover the causes of his failure. In either case, he will know more about speaking before he tries again, and his effectiveness as a speaker will continue to grow over the years. Speech is an intellectual discipline, and those who would speak well cannot ignore that fact.

Speech is a democratic process. The intelligent exercise of the privilege of free speech is basic to a democratic society. We do not feel that all ideas or viewpoints are of equal worth. Some may contribute to the development and improvement of human life. Others may serve to injure and destroy. No individual, however, has the right to distinguish arbitrarily between ideas and to tell the rest of us what we must believe. Each citizen has the opportunity and responsibility to hear all sides and to select what he considers best. The preference of the majority may then become the principle governing all of us in certain areas of mutual concern.

This democratic position is quite distinct from what might be called the authoritarian view of truth. The authoritarian view places the truth in the past, something already discovered and fully understood in a given case. All other ideas are then worthless, for the truth is known. It need now only be taught and protected from error. Some elite group, guardians of the truth, must pass judgment on the rest of us, censoring what we write or speak in order to make sure that only the truth is communicated and that error has been silenced.

This authoritarian view leaves little room for rhetoric. Why should we try to persuade one another about the good, the beautiful, and the just if the proper conclusions are already fixed? There is little point in addressing an audience on the proposition that two plus two equal four. Discussion and persuasion take place in those areas of life in which the truth is unknown or uncertain. If the word of some dictator is the truth, then he should talk, and the rest of us need only listen and obey.

The democratic viewpoint, on the other hand, may be regarded as locating the truth in the future. We seek the truth; we work toward it. The truth that we know now is partial; we look forward to the day when we shall have complete knowledge. Our views are tentative, subject to review and to change. We may have convictions which we firmly believe to be true and which we try to persuade others to accept, but we would not force our beliefs upon another person. Even our most cherished opinions are held humbly, with honest regard for those who may disagree with us and with ultimate respect reserved for God, who alone is really Truth.

This democratic view, and our various social and political institutions which embody it, must rest, in part, upon the freedom of speech and the press. If no individual or group has a monopoly on the truth, then we should all join the common effort to find the best solutions to the problems that trouble us. Each individual has some bit of knowledge or wisdom. Let him contribute the understanding that he has achieved; let the rest of us subject his ideas to analysis and criticism from our various points of view. Ultimately, we can expect to find goodness and justice in government or in society to the extent that we are freely able to exchange ideas and to subject each idea to examination and discussion. The more strict the limits placed on freedom of expression, the poorer the chances that human progress will be achieved.

The argument for freedom of speech is strong; it rests upon two major assumptions. The first is our faith that in the nature of things truth is stronger and superior to error. We cannot really prove that this faith is justified. We may rest it upon our belief in the goodness of God or upon our observations of order in the universe. Nevertheless, we suppose that this assumption is correct, that truth is more powerful than the big lie, that right, properly represented, shall always prevail over wrong.

But will right always receive proper representation? The second major assumption which underlies our belief in freedom of speech is the belief that in any discussion truth will be as effectively presented as is error. Truth spoken in a listless, halting whisper cannot compete with a lie broadcast with all the power of Adolph Hitler's propaganda machine. Truth supported by arguments which are illogical and confused in statement cannot be expected to withstand the persuasive sophistries of error.

Our first assumption concerned the nature of the universe. We believe that everything is so organized that right will prevail. Whether our faith be correct or not, nothing that mankind can do will alter the situation. Our second assumption, however, pertains to the actions of human beings. We believe that speakers or writers who advocate the good, the true, and the just will have the skill and will to devote the necessary time and effort for promoting their causes.

None of us can determine truth ahead of time in order to make plans to present it effectively. Rather, we must prepare each man to advance his ideas in the most persuasive manner possible, even though we know he will sometimes be wrong. Let no viewpoint be poorly represented. Then the inherent power of truth will have the opportunity to make it victorious in the long run. A democratic society allows freedom of expression for all and a corresponding responsibility, that we all dedicate ourselves to express the truth, as we understand it, with the greatest force and clarity of which we are capable. In so doing, we make our contributions to our democratic society through the intelligent exercise of our privilege of free speech.

SOME BASIC RULES

These primary considerations give rise to a number of specific rules of procedure which govern the various activities involved in the study of public speaking. These rules must be followed if the reader is to receive the benefits which he has a right to expect from this book and its assignments. Some of these rules may make the act of speaking seem more difficult, and you may know many experienced speakers who violate many of them. Nevertheless, the student who breaks a rule frustrates some of the careful planning demanded by this text and robs himself of some of his opportunity for personal growth. Be sure that you understand the meaning of each rule and the reasons for it. Then follow the rules to the best of your ability.

1. *Speak extemporaneously.* Prepare your speeches carefully, but do not write out or memorize them. The only exceptions will occur later, after you have greater experience and have acquired some of the skills needed in the production of the written speech. You will find that this book includes a written speech in the final assignment. For the present, the process of writing a speech would be too time-consuming. It could also lead to more serious problems. If you started writing speeches now, you would probably transfer your present literary style into speech composition. To do so would be a serious mistake, for your oral style should be quite distinct from your written style. You should never attempt to write a speech until your oral style has become fixed as a result of a great deal of practice in speaking. Furthermore, the written speech tends to make the act of speaking an exercise in remembering rather than a participation in the real process of communication. Don't write out the speech. Have your main ideas clearly in mind. Then just tell them to your listeners in the same way that you would converse with a friend.

2. *Prepare all speeches carefully, unless an impromptu speech is required.* The term "extemporaneous" refers to a type of speech delivery, not to the amount of preparation a speech has received. The fact that a speech is not written means that the preparation must be even more intensive. Know what you are going to discuss. Get the facts. Organize them into some sort of pattern that both you and your audience can remember. Practice the speech, out loud. Try it again and again, until the words begin to flow and you can really say what you mean. Prepare!

A truly impromptu speech is probably a rare event. Most successful speeches that seem to be given without preparation are made on topics thoroughly familiar to the speaker, and about which he has often spoken. Thus he has a great supply of material which can readily be adapted to fit the case at hand. The only alternative is to speak in vague generalities and say nothing, a procedure rarely classified as successful speaking!

3. *Give each assignment your best efforts.* Never regard them as too easy, unimportant, silly, or "not for me." Granted, these assignments are planned for beginners, while you may have had a great deal of experience. The assignments, however, are speeches, and each one can be a challenge to you to use all of your intelligence and experience in both preparation and delivery. In doing so, you will find that you profit even more than the beginner working to fulfill the same assignment. Furthermore, you should never regard any speech opportunity, in class or otherwise, as nothing more than an excuse for you to display your overall talent as a speaker. We speak to communicate worthwhile information and ideas. Each assignment is directed toward making you more effective in communication, and each one will emphasize some specific aspect of your task. Understand each point of emphasis, and do your best to develop that particular talent. You will find each assignment both stimulating and helpful, no matter how extensive your past experience as a speaker may have been.

4. *Take every opportunity to speak.* The only way to learn to speak effectively is to do it. Your assignment to speak on a given day is an important obligation. The politician must meet his speaking engagements or expect a number of disgruntled voters. A teacher must appear before his class at the scheduled time and place, ready to present his lecture. Likewise, the minister cannot ask his congregation to come back some other Sunday to hear him. A conscientious speaker is probably never quite satisfied with the preparation that he has been able to give any speech. Whether he happens to be in the mood or not, the time comes when the speech is to be given, and he must be there and do it. Begin now to face these realities. Prepare each speech to the best of your ability; then speak when called upon.

5. *Be objective in giving and accepting criticism.* No one can correct his faults until he becomes aware of them. Adverse criticism thus becomes essential to speech improvement. However, speech and personality are closely related. Sometimes speakers feel that any mention of faults in their speech must be a personal attack. Then they become rigid and defensive and unable to profit from suggestions that are offered with only helpful intent. Be objective about your speech. It is only a piece of workmanship which you have produced, as you might build a table or a chair. None of these things are so well made that they cannot be improved; criticism gives you the opportunity for improvement. Don't impute motives to your critic. Assume that he is kindly and has only your best interests at heart. Then you will be able to accept and to evaluate intelligently this criticism and to profit thereby. No matter what the critic's original motive might have been, you will become a better speaker. Learn to give and to receive criticism with the same gracious spirit.

6. *Listen to other speakers.* Even on those occasions when your primary concern is with the speech which you must give, common courtesy requires you to give other speakers the same thoughtful attention that you hope to receive when you speak. However, you should also be curious about the manner in which other individuals meet and solve the same problems that face you as a speaker. Pay particular attention to the criticisms that other speakers receive. These remarks may help you to become aware of the same faults in your own speaking. Don't become so lost in the other speaker's message that you forget to note the techniques which he uses in conveying it. The listening assignments in this text will help you to remember and to profit most from the listening you do.

7. *Give each of your speeches time to grow.* Collect your thoughts and ideas over a period of time, if you possibly can. Last-minute preparation is inefficient preparation. Get your basic ideas in mind as soon as possible after you have accepted any

speaking engagement. Then your subconscious mind will contribute to the development of the speech as you go about your various other activities. All of your reading, listening, and everyday experiences will contribute to your speech if you know the basic ideas that you plan to develop. Final preparation then becomes an easy matter of selection from the great stock of material which you will have accumulated. Begin early, distribute your preparation, and save time.

The secret is to get started. Decide on the topic for your next speech as soon as you have finished the last one. Some ministers follow the wise practice that they will not retire on Sunday night until they have chosen the topic and text for next Sunday's sermon. Once you have determined the general area in which you will speak, don't shift. Other topics may occur to you; make a note of them for the future, but don't let them tempt you to develop them this time. Spread your preparation of each speech over the full extent of your preparation period. Give your speech time to grow.

8. *Speak from experience.* The audience wants to know your ideas. If they wanted the thoughts of someone else, they would listen to someone else. You have the right to speak only in those areas in which, by reason of long experience or special study, you have become a semi-expert. Avoid the speech which gives the audience a little general knowledge in some broad area; it adds nothing to what they already know. Avoid the speech which merely repeats the content of some printed sermon or magazine article; others can read these things for themselves. Give your own personal ideas and beliefs.

This principle, which applies to any type of speaking, applies particularly to preaching. The gospel which is to be preached is essentially a personal witness. Notice the definition of the gospel found in I Corinthians 15, closing with the words, "Last of all he was seen of me also." Read carefully the various sermons contained in the New Testament. The Sermon on the Mount is filled with "Ye have heard that it was said . . . but I say unto you." Peter's sermon on the day of Pentecost (Acts 2) begins with a contemporary event and ends with the resurrection, of which "we all are witnesses." Stephen's sermon (Acts 7) begins with Abraham but ends with "the Just One; of whom ye have been now the betrayers and murderers." Paul's sermons seem to center on the account of his own conversion. Even his least successful sermon, the one delivered in Athens (Acts 17), ends with his own witness to the resurrection of Christ. Great preaching is primarily a sincere account of the speaker's personal faith. Always speak from experience, particularly when you stand in the pulpit.

9. *Always have an outline*—either in your head, on paper, or both. This outline need not be a formidable document; it is primarily a list of things you plan to talk about in the order in which you propose to present them to the audience. It is like a grocery list giving the items you expect to pick up in the supermarket in the order that is most efficient for your shopping. It is like the blueprint or plan of a house that you propose to build. No good builder would start a house and then revise his plan in the process of building if he could possibly avoid doing so. Instead, he will prepare an architectural drawing and make his revisions on paper where changes can be made easily and inexpensively. In a similar manner, the speaker plans his speech. His ideas are listed in brief form on his outline—his blueprint. There, changes and revisions can be made easily and efficiently. Only after an outline has been completed and perfected is the speaker really ready to practice the delivery of the speech. If a speech manuscript is necessary, the writing should begin *only* when the outline has been completed. Speech assignments in this book will include sample outlines for you to follow as you work to master the technique.

The impromptu speech varies from these general principles only in degree. As a speaker comes to his feet, he has in mind a point or two that he wants to make. This mental list constitutes his outline. It will lack the polish that careful preparation over a period of days or weeks would give it, and it will also be subject to additions and changes as the speaker talks.

Many speakers also prepare a brief form of the outline to have before them on the pulpit or speaker's stand as they speak. This form of the outline is usually termed the speaker's "notes." Do not confuse "notes" and "outline." The former is an abbreviation of the latter. The outline should be complete, containing every idea that the speaker will present, and should constitute a detailed blueprint of the speech. The notes may be as brief as the speaker's memory will permit.

Since notes may be distracting to both speaker and audience, many speakers prefer to commit the outline to memory and to dispense with notes entirely. Such a procedure has much to commend it if the speaker has trained himself to rely on his memory and to cope with emergency situations that arise when his mind unexpectedly goes blank. All of us admire the freedom of the speaker who can talk without notes. He is free to gesture since his hands are not filled with papers or busy shuffling those obtrusive little cards which many speakers use. He is free to move about since he is not dependent upon the pulpit or stand which holds his notes. He is free to maintain eye contact with his audience since it is not necessary for him to look down at his notes.

The ability to speak without notes is not some miraculous gift of a photographic memory but a simple skill which any speaker can develop. It requires careful preparation, for an illogical or rambling speech will be difficult for both speaker and audience to remember. It requires repeated practice, for good memory means drill and overlearning. Above all, the ability to speak without notes requires the simple courage to throw away the notes and to depend upon one's memory to supply the speech which has been prepared. Speaking without notes is not some advanced technique which you can begin to acquire after you have mastered the art of public speaking. It is a skill which is developed most easily at the beginning, while you are learning to speak. If you will begin now, making every speech without notes, learning from your failures, overcoming the moments of difficulty and embarrassment, and never giving up, the skill can be yours. Begin now by making the rule that, while you will always have an outline, you will never use notes while speaking. You will not be sorry.

10. *Complete each assignment accurately and on time.* If you are working in a group, it is important that you maintain the pace of the entire group. The assignments are not in random order. Each speaking assignment builds on those that have gone before, and the listening assignments are coordinated with the speaking assignments. Thus the entire class must move steadily from one assignment to the next. For any one individual to fall behind would disrupt the concentration of the entire class on the assignment being studied.

If you plan to follow this text by yourself, without the discipline of class assignments, the regularity of your work becomes even more important. Set a schedule for each assignment and maintain it religiously. Procrastination is the great enemy of self-study courses. Defer an assignment for one week, and you'll find it easy to wait a second week—and then a third. The best intentions are forgotten, and the work is never done at all. A schedule of two weeks per assignment should be reasonable. Hold to it and allow yourself no exceptions.

SOME SPECIFIC PROCEDURES

Each assignment in this text assumes a regular, orderly pro cedure on the part of the student. The suggestions that follow are offered in order to encourage you in methods that are the easiest, most efficient, and most beneficial for you if you are to achieve the specific objectives of each project and the general objectives of the course. Familiarize yourself with the various steps now; look back to them frequently as you proceed. Many of these ideas should prove helpful in areas other than public speaking.

Procedures for assigned papers

1. Locate the assigned books. Verify the author, title, edition, and date. Be sure that chapters and page numbers correspond with the assignment. Other editions of a given book may also be helpful, but chapter and page numbers will not necessarily correspond with the information you have.

2. Check the writing assignment so that you can read intelligently with a specific problem or problems in mind.

3. Take notes as you read.

4. Let your interest guide you to additional readings not mentioned in this book. Many texts have other sources listed at the end of each chapter. You will find other books and articles in footnotes or within the discussion itself.

5. When your reading for a specific topic has been completed, prepare a brief outline for the paper you intend to write.

6. Follow that outline in writing a first draft of your paper. Be sure that your discussion follows the assignment. Note these specific suggestions:

   a. Observe the difference between "discuss" and "list" in these assignments. A list is simply a number of separate items placed in order. A discussion is an extended exploration and elaboration of a given area of knowledge.

   b. Cite your sources. Give credit for the ideas that come from your reading. The source quoted, directly or indirectly, should be given in a footnote. To claim credit for ideas you have taken from another is dishonest.

   c. Add your own ideas. Indicate your reaction to what the various writers say. Compare, criticize, elaborate from your own thinking and experience. The paper should represent your conclusions on the basis of your reading and whatever experience you may have had. You are not to be merely a recording machine compiling information from the various sources.

7. Revise and rewrite as many times as necessary. Someone has said, "There is no such thing as good writing; there is only good rewriting."

8. Check spelling and punctuation. If you are uncertain as to the spelling of any word, use the dictionary. Not everyone can be an expert speller, but everyone can be industrious and conscientious enough to look up the words.

9. Prepare the final draft. The following checklist applies to almost all written work done by college undergraduates.

a. General form? Follow some standard style sheet, especially in such matters as footnotes and bibliography. One suggested reference is: Kate L. Turabian, *A Manual for Writers of Term Papers, Theses, and Dissertations* (Rev. ed.; Chicago: The University of Chicago Press, 1955). Others may perfer to follow *The MLA Style Sheet,* available from the Treasurer of the Modern Language Association of America, 6 Washington Square North, New York 3, New York.

b. Appearance and legibility? Never submit work done in pencil or on both sides of the paper to any college instructor, or to any editor for that matter. A typed paper is preferred.

c. Proper margins? You should leave at least 1½ inches on the left and at least 1 inch on the other three sides.

d. Your name? Be certain your name appears on the first page. Many writers also put their names or initials next to the page numbers on the other pages.

e. Title? Be certain that the title of the paper and some indication of the assignment appear on the first page.

f. Pages? Be certain that the pages are properly numbered, in order, and securely fastened.

g. Proofreading? Give your paper a final check for typographical errors. One good method is to read the paper backward, word for word. Another method is to give the paper a series of readings, concentrating each time on some particular problem: Read aloud for (1) general style; (2) spelling; (3) the use of the apostrophe with the possessive; (4) agreement of pronouns and antecedents; (5) agreement of subjects and verbs; (6) incomplete sentences.

10. Submit the paper when it is due, or earlier if possible.

Procedures for assigned speeches

1. Determine your speech subject early. You should have a subject in mind for your next speech before the end of the day on which you last spoke.

2. Prepare a work sheet which lists all of the ideas and information which you have been able to accumulate pertaining to this speech subject. Begin the process of evaluation as you eliminate items that obviously don't belong. Get the material which is left into some logical order. You will probably find gaps in your knowledge of this subject which will force you to consult an encyclopedia, almanac, or some of the writings that others have produced about this same thing. Do not attempt to do a complete job of research on this subject. Such a project should not be necessary since you are speaking from experience. On the other hand, do not let these gaps of knowledge discourage you and cause you to change subjects. Do not change at this stage of your preparation. Rather, look for some aspect of the subject which you are qualified to discuss. You should complete this work sheet and be ready for the next step at least two days prior to the time you are to speak.

3. Prepare the outline of your speech. Check the assignment to be certain your outline fits the requirements in every detail. Remember that the outline is primarily a list of the things you intend to discuss in the order in which you plan to discuss them. However, your list should be complete enough that you could virtually reproduce the same speech a year later, working from the outline alone. Revise your outline if necessary. The final

copy should be neat, legible, and free from errors in spelling and punctuation.

4. Practice your speech aloud. Try it first with your outline in hand to aid your memory. As you become familiar with the content, practice the speech without reference to the outline. Avoid repeating the same language in the expression of your ideas as you practice. Your aim should be to vary the wording as widely as possible in order to achieve fluency when you finally deliver the speech to an audience. The greater the variety of expressions that you practice, the smaller the chance of "blocking" when you speak and your mind is unable to find some particular turn of phrase. This period of practice may also lead you to make further changes in your outline as you add new ideas or rearrange your material.

5. Make the final preparations for delivering your speech. The following checklist should be valuable, whether the speech is a class assignment, a sermon, or an address for some other occasion:

   a. The final, complete copy of your outline. Your instructor may wish to see this material. In any event, you should preserve it in your files.

   b. The notes, if you are able to use notes, which you will take to the speaker's stand with you.

   c. The details of the speaking engagement, to be certain you understand the time, the place, the occasion, the audience, the person who is to introduce you.

   d. Any additional materials you may need. You may have cards or leaflets to distribute after the speech or pictures or charts to use in giving the speech itself.

   e. Your dress and general appearance. Do you look clean, neat, unobtrusively fashionable, appropriately dressed for the audience and occasion?

6. Deliver the speech as planned. Arrive early, locate the individual in charge, learn all you can about where you are to sit, how you are to be introduced, and your place in the total pro-

gram. You should also feel free to vary from your plan as the occasion demands. Remember, you are engaging in an act of communication with the audience, not putting on a show for them. Adapt your remarks to what has gone before, to what you see or hear as you speak, and to whatever is to follow. The matter of time limits may prove particularly awkward. Perhaps you were told to speak for twenty minutes, concluding your remarks at 8:30. Something went wrong, however, and the chairman finally introduced you at 8:25. Under such circumstances, you should be able to condense your speech and to give the gist of it in about ten minutes.

7. Evaluate the speech on your permanent outline. Keep a record of the time, place, and audience to whom you gave the speech, plus any observations you may have and any changes that you would make in using that material again.

You have now begun the study of public speaking. The rewards you reap will not be in proportion to your present talents but in proportion to your investment in preparation and practice. Few other courses can offer you as much in terms of personal satisfaction, personality development, and improved social relationships. What you will gain is now up to you.

PROJECTS AND ASSIGNMENTS*

Supplementary Reading in the Speech Texts

Blankenship and Wilhoit, *Selected Readings in Public Speaking,* Ch. 1: The Nature of Communication.

Sarett, *Basic Principles of Speech,* Ch. 1: The Nature and Study of Speech; Ch. 2: Principles of Effective Speech; Ch. 4: Communication: The Presentation of Ideas.

* Additional readings for each chapter will be found in the appendix, p. 199. For complete information on books listed, see the bibliographies.

Wilson and Arnold, *Public Speaking as a Liberal Art,* Ch. 1: The Art of Public Speaking; Ch. 2: Heritage: The Evolution of Rhetorical Theory.

Supplementary Reading in the Preaching Texts

Davis, *Design for Preaching,* Ch. 1: Substance and Form.

Farmer, *The Servant of the Word,* Ch. 2: The I-Thou Relationship; Ch. 3: Preaching as Personal Encounter.

Jones, *Principles and Practice of Preaching,* Ch. 1: The Importance of Preaching; Ch. 2: The Purpose of Preaching; Ch. 3: The Preacher's Part in His Preaching.

Writing Assignment

Discuss one of the following topics:
1. Preaching as a Type of Public Speaking
2. Great Preachers Are Born, Not Made
3. Speaking as a Communicative Act
4. Speech in a Democratic Society
5. Distinctive Aspects of Preaching
6. A Wise Man Prepares to Preach

Speaking Assignment

Prepare and deliver a speech in which you introduce yourself to the audience. Include the following items:
1. Your name
2. Your education
3. Your vocation (present or planned)
4. Your favorite hobby or hobbies
5. Your personal reactions to the study of public speaking

Listening Assignment

Take notes on the other speeches of self-introduction that you hear. Pay particular attention to the following items:
1. The name
2. The one thing about each speaker which is most interesting to you.

Be sure you preserve these notes, for they will provide part of the material for your next speaking assignment.

2

Your Speech Resources

Speech begins with an idea. You speak because you have something to say. You feel that your thoughts will inform, influence, or entertain your listeners. The accomplishment of even one such purpose, you feel, will be of benefit, both to your listeners and to yourself. Hence you struggle to express that idea, in oral or written symbols, to "put it over" in such a way that your hearers or readers will comprehend it and appreciate it as you do.

All of us have a supply of ideas that we value in this way, ideas that others need to know. Consider, for instance:

People. Many sermons have been preached about Bible personalities or about the great saints of Christian history. You may not have known Peter, Paul, Augustine, Luther, or Wesley, but you know others who could be just as inspiring to us. We need to know such personalities. The story of that doctor or minister or teacher may be of real help and interest to us.

Work. No one understands your job as well as you do. Explain it to us. We may know the process, but your feelings about that process are important. A great Teacher once attracted followers by promising to turn fishermen into fishers of men. You can help your hearers to grow by reminding them of the divine potential in even the common and ordinary tasks.

Hobbies. Again, the sharing of appreciations is important. If you can get us to see that some pastime which we thought was silly has real importance, you contribute to the enrichment of our lives and to our understanding of other people.

Family. All of us are involved in complex social relationships which pose problems we never completely solve. Your own family background may furnish insights invaluable to the rest of us.

Convictions. Probably no one else in all the world believes just as you do on every subject. Share your convictions with us; your message will be unique. The very basis of Christian preaching lies in this area. True preaching is not the process of telling other people what they ought to do. Rather, it is the preacher's personal witness to his convictions about what God has done for us in Christ. Your discussion may not persuade the rest of us to hold convictions identical with yours; no speaker is as effective as all that. But if you can broaden our viewpoints, soften our prejudices, and make us more understanding people, you will have accomplished a great deal.

Perhaps you are afraid that you have nothing new or different to contribute in any of these areas. Good! A healthy fear of talking without saying anything will save you from making some bad speeches. A vague, half-informed idea about an interesting person or a religious conviction is only a starting point, not a speech. An idea doesn't become a speech until you have thought about it, studied it, and made yourself an expert in that area. It doesn't become a speech until you have far more information than you could possibly express in the time available to you.

The next step, then, in working from an idea to a speech is to supplement your basic idea. This process begins immediately after you think of a possible speech idea and continues throughout the preparation of the speech until that moment when your message is actually delivered. Specific aspects of this total process will include such activities as the following:

1. *Think.* Try to recall all that you have known and have experienced about this idea. Reason from cause to effect and from effect to cause. Ask yourself: how? who? what? where? when? why? Utilize your subconscious. Think about this matter over a period of time at various odd moments. You will find that additional ideas will come to you when you least expect them. This process of thinking should precede the other methods of accumulating ideas, for your own background of thought and experience may serve to improve the efficiency of subsequent research.

2. *Listen.* Any idea that you wish to discuss is probably the subject of many speeches and conversations. This fact should not deter you from having your say. Rather, it offers you a rich store of resources that you cannot afford to ignore. Give attention to other speakers in your class, to your minister on Sunday morning, to that news commentator on television. Some of these speakers may be talking about completely different subjects, but their remarks will set off a train of thought in your mind which will offer a new insight into the subject which interests you. Some ministers have been known to establish formal discussion groups within their congregations to engage in free discussion of next Sunday's sermon text. Perhaps you could introduce your subject into a casual conversation in order to note the reactions and profit from the ideas of your friends.

3. *Observe.* Scenes and events may suggest ideas to those trained and oriented to catch the suggestion. Sometimes the connection is obvious as in the case of a highway accident that you observe while gathering materials for a speech on highway safety and the moral aspects of safe driving. At other times the relationship is not so clear. Perhaps you see a squirrel gathering nuts for the winter, and you relate this scene to a speech you are planning on laying up treasure in heaven where moth and rust do not consume. Some of the great messages of religious history

have sprung from simple observations such as these. Jeremiah was watching a potter at work when the word of the Lord came to him and he saw the likeness between Israel and the potter's clay. Jesus used his observations of a farmer sowing his grain to teach great truths about the word of God. Your own abilities to see more than the obvious and to grasp the implications of what you see can be improved with practice. Have the idea that concerns you clearly in mind and try to relate the various events of everyday life to some aspect of your proposed speech. You will find your stock of speech materials growing rapidly.

4. *Interview.* When you want specific information and can arrange a meeting with one who has it, schedule an interview. Prepare your questions beforehand and have them clearly in mind so that the interview won't waste time—yours or that of the person you are meeting. The interview is not a method of beginning your research but a method of supplementing your store of facts. Let your expert do the talking. Concentrate on him; take notes only when you must. You can put the ideas down in writing elsewhere when your writing will not be a distraction. Be sure, however, that your conclusions are recorded in permanent form as soon as the interview is over, while the facts are still fresh in your mind. You may also want to talk to the expert again, perhaps by telephone, in order to verify specific items or to get permission to quote if you expect to cite his direct words. In conducting an interview, you have a particular responsibility to be courteous, to arrive and leave promptly according to your original arrangements, and to respect the feelings of your authority at all times.

5. *Correspond.* If you can't go to see the individual who has the facts, write to him. Make your request clear and specific. Don't impose upon his time by asking for information which is available elsewhere; you have no right to ask another person to do your library work for you. Don't ask for too many specific things. If you request too much, the one reading your letter will become impatient and discouraged; your letter will promptly

find its place in his wastebasket. Phrase your request in such a way that the reader will understand your need for the information and will be motivated to want to help you. Above all, don't forget to enclose that stamped, self-addressed envelope for the reply.

6. *Read.* Understand the true nature of a library. Too many people regard it as a forbidding temple of silence devoted to the meaningless labors of extracting words from books. A greater distortion of the truth is hard to imagine. In actuality, a library is a great deepfreeze which contains in frozen form most of the great minds in the history of mankind. These frozen minds are the books. The process of thawing them out and restoring them to life again is called "reading." If you know where to look (and libraries are arranged thoughtfully and logically) and if your library is large enough, you can come in contact with almost every great intelligence, past or present. You can interview the experts, bringing them to life again and hearing what they have to say on all of the important subjects that have concerned the human race. Few projects can be as stimulating and exciting as library research.

Each library will have certain guides to help you locate the material you need. Learn how to use the card catalog, the general and special encyclopedias, the lists of books in print, the indexes of articles in periodicals, the collections of biographical information, statistical information, and quotations, and the various dictionaries. If you have problems, the librarian will be glad to help you.

These six processes will enable you to come in contact with new information and ideas. This material, however, will mean nothing to your thinking or speaking until you assimilate it, until you relate these ideas to the concepts which you already possess. Assimilation will require some effort on your part. You cannot turn the pages of a book hoping that ideas will jump at you any more than you can sleep with the book under your pillow and expect to absorb thoughts by osmosis. You must interact and react to the thinking which is presented to you in that book.

If you have begun your research properly, with a topic clearly in mind and your own ideas assembled first, you should have no trouble in assimilating new materials. You have a basic viewpoint in mind; hence you can relate new ideas to a center of your own experience. You are working to structure a speech; thus you will fit new ideas into a pattern so that relationships stand out clearly and the material is easier to remember. Nevertheless, some other specific suggestions may help to make you more efficient in the assimilation of new thoughts and information.

1. *Prepare yourself physically.* Shut out noise and distractions. Have a private study spot where intruders will be at a minimum. Discover your own best time for study, when you seem to operate most efficiently, and devote that hour to your work each day. Remember, you cannot stay in one position or place indefinitely. Give yourself a break; walk around for a few minutes or get yourself a snack and then return to the work.

2. *Prepare yourself mentally.* Motivate yourself by reminding yourself of the importance of this study, of this book or this class. Notice the meaning that these ideas have for you; relate them to what you already know; become conscious of differences of approach or viewpoint. Look for meaning. The more you know about any subject, the better prepared you are to hear, evaluate, and remember discussions of that subject. Therefore, mentally review what you know about any area before listening or reading in that area. The more you learn, the better you are prepared for your next learning experience.

3. *Prepare yourself emotionally.* Speakers work in areas of controversy and disagreement, where feelings often run high. You will need to acquaint yourself with sides of the question other than your own. Don't let your own viewpoint block your understanding of other positions. Try to rule the question "Do I

agree?" out of your mind for the time being. Ask yourself: What is the man saying? What are his assumptions? What does he believe? What is his evidence? Your effort is to understand the other writer or speaker, not to argue with him. In other words, you must be open-minded. You need not surrender any of your own convictions. As someone has said, you need not be so open-minded that your brains fall out. In the act of analytical listening or reading, however, you should suspend your beliefs relative to the speaker or writer and his subject in order to facilitate your grasp of what he says. Remember, even a slight emotional reaction to the personality or the subject matter may blind you to the true content of the message.

4. *Get started.* The hardest part of any period of study is the beginning. All of us can think of a thousand little things that need doing which somehow keep us away from what we know we ought to do. Don't wait for perfect conditions for study; make the best of what you have and get to work. Don't wait for that extended block of time to devote to your reading—you may wait forever. Utilize the ten minutes you have between appointments or at some other odd period. Some people motivate themselves by setting deadlines; they may decide, for instance, to read two chapters before going to lunch or to write two pages each day. Others offer themselves a reward, perhaps a bite of candy after finishing each chapter. Still others find they begin more easily if they do the more pleasant reading first. If you are writing, the first sentence is often the most difficult. Don't be afraid to put something on paper. You can always revise and discard this early material later if it does not come up to your standards. The important thing is to begin.

5. *Follow a study method.* The initials **P–Q–R–S–T** can remind you of one good procedure.

P—*Preview* the assignment. Scan quickly what you are to read. Note the chapter and paragraph headings. Get the general idea of the material. Begin the book with the table of contents. Try to grasp the manner in which the author expects to proceed.

Q—*Question* yourself. What information do you expect to get from the material you have surveyed? What would you really like to find out?

R—*Read* the material. Try to find out the answers to your questions. Note the way in which the author has organized the material. Don't hurry. Your reading rate should vary with the difficulty of the material which you are reading. Don't try to set a speed record in reading difficult material, especially if you want to grasp and remember the content.

S—*State* what you have read in your own words. Go through the material, point by point, and see if you can summarize what the author said. If not, reread that section.

T—*Test* your memory after an interval of time. Go through the material the next day, point by point, and see if you can summarize the author's views.

The same procedures will also serve for listening to another speaker. They are especially important in taking notes on a lecture.

P—*Preview* the lecture. What do you know about the speaker and his topic? Prepare your notes by listing the time, date, occasion, audience, and speaker.

Q—*Question* yourself. How would you develop that topic if you were going to discuss it? What areas would you discuss? What viewpoint would you advocate? What issues would you consider basic? How would you adapt your discussion to this audience and occasion?

R—*Read;* that is, listen to the speaker. Discover how he actually handles the situation. Maintain your objectivity. Don't let your disagreement with the speaker's viewpoint or your dislike for his methods make you deaf to what he is actually saying. Pay attention to:

THE IDEAS. What specific information did the speaker have?

What were his arguments? How did he clarify his ideas? What evidence supported his arguments?

THE STRUCTURE. How were his ideas arranged? How were they related to one another and to the speaker's general purpose in speaking?

THE LANGUAGE. How did the speaker express himself in words? Was he clear? Did he create images and move the feelings of his audience?

THE MEMORY. Was the speaker familiar with his material?

THE DELIVERY. Was his voice pleasing in quality, adequate in volume, interesting in its rate and pitch variety? Did he enunciate clearly? Were his movements appropriate and coordinated with his words?

S—*State* in your own words what you hear. The notes that you take will be a paraphrase of the speaker's important points.

T—*Test* your memory. Try to summarize the speaker's views after the lecture is over.

6. *Take notes.* This process is probably more important in listening than in reading, but you should make it a habit in either case. Don't depend upon your unaided memory; get everything down on paper. The following suggestions may help:

Listen. The process of taking notes is not a substitute for paying attention. Read or listen carefully, noting the relationship of ideas, getting the entire sweep of the lecture or chapter.

Transcribe. Get the ideas down on paper, as quickly and with as much detail as you can. You won't have time to make a neat outline with proper headings and indentations. Indicate relationships by such devices as drawing arrows, indenting, underlining. Neatness doesn't count; completeness does!

Document. Carefully identify the source of your notes. Get the time, place, subject, and speaker for the lectures you hear. Get complete publication data on any book or article you read. Nothing wastes time more than looking up an article the second time in order to get the page number for a bibliography.

Review. As soon as possible after a lecture or after reading a chapter, review your notes on that material. While your memory is fresh, you will be able to amplify passages that do not seem clear in your notes.

File. Develop your own filing system for the subjects that concern you or adopt one of the commercial systems on the market. Notes that are lost or that are buried in a paper box somewhere are of little use to anyone.

7. *Reinforce your learning.* Go over the material again and again so you will remember it. Utilize as many of your senses as possible. Underline in colored pencil. Speak the material out loud; even sing the ideas or draw cartoons about them if you are able. If possible, review at night, just before you go to sleep. Don't leave everything for the last minute; review constantly and regularly.

8. *Discipline yourself.* You will never become an adequate scholar by waiting until the mood strikes you or by depending upon others to motivate you to study. Your speeches will come from your reservoir of ideas and information. Keeping that reservoir full requires your constant attention and industry. Set study projects for yourself in which you work to master some area of knowledge. Break each project into subordinate areas and assign deadlines for each section. Don't let a day pass that you fail to accomplish the goal you set for that day.

Above all, the good speaker is a man who knows what he is talking about. He is an educated individual, not just in the sense of having attended school and received the proper credits and degrees, but in the sense of being able to make mature judgments on the basis of a breadth of knowledge. He is dedicated to intellectual growth, and he knows how to use the basic tools of investigation to fill the gaps in his understanding. He knows when to talk; he knows when to keep still. But when he talks, he receives the respectful attention of the thoughtful, for they know he has earned it. As far as the content of his message is concerned, he is the ideal orator—the good man speaking.

PROJECTS AND ASSIGNMENTS

Supplementary Reading in the Speech Texts

Adler, *How to Read a Book,* Ch. 7: From Many Rules to One Habit;
　Ch. 8: Catching on from the Title; Ch. 9: Seeing the Skeleton.
Brigance, *Speech: Its Techniques and Disciplines in a Free Society,*
　Ch. 10: Earning the Right to Speak.

Supplementary Reading in the Preaching Texts

Garrison, *The Preacher and His Audience,* Ch. 6: Sources of Material
Jones, *Principles and Practice of Preaching,* Ch. 13: Accumulating Sermon Ideas; Ch. 14: Planning Ahead.

Writing Assignment

Discuss one of the following topics:
　1. A Speaker's Evaluation of One Particular Library
　2. The Minister's Personal Library—Its Purpose, Value, and Content
　3. A Comparison of Preaching and Public Speaking in Regard to Sources of Material
　4. Taking Notes Efficiently
　5. Research Techniques for the Pulpit
　6. The Value of a City Library to Sermon Preparation

Speaking Assignment

You are to conduct an interview with another member of the class (assigned by the instructor) to get the necessary information; then you are to make a speech to introduce him to the rest of the class. The speech should be a short one (not over 3 or 4 minutes) but should include all of the following information:

1. His name, including any nickname. (Be sure the audience will be able to spell it, pronounce it, and remember it.)
2. His home town. Give a little of his background, including schools attended or previous jobs.
3. His future plans. Such items as his college major and his vocational objective should be included here.
4. His recreations. Include information about his hobbies and any of his favorite occupations apart from his present or future vocation.
5. His speaking potential. On the basis of your knowledge of this person, indicate some subject on which you feel he is qualified to speak, a subject that you would enjoy hearing him discuss and on which you feel he would make a contribution to the average listener. (Note: You are not to evaluate his abilities as a speaker on this subject or any other. Rather, you are to suggest a subject which you would like to have him discuss at some future date.)

Arrange these items in any order that you wish, but be certain to include them all. Prepare an outline which indicates the order that you plan to use; then follow that order.

Alternative speaking assignment: Make a similar speech of introduction, including the same points, but introducing some personality of the Bible to your audience.

Listening Assignment

Listen carefully to all the other speakers as they fulfill the speaking assignment for this chapter. Keep a record of the following items for each:

1. The name of each speaker
2. The name of the person being introduced
3. Your personal evaluation of the speech subject suggested for the person being introduced (item 5 in the speaking assignment). Do you consider it significant? interesting? not really important? a complete waste of time?

Try to keep your evaluation from being too highly individual. Certain subjects may seem insignificant to you because of certain experiences in your own life. Don't let some unusual background color your judgment too much, but think in terms of your class or of an average adult audience in your city. What would be the attitude of these people toward a well-prepared, thoughtful presentation of this subject if they heard it?

3

Your Speech Subject

By this time, you probably have a number of ideas that you would like to discuss with any audience that will listen. Perhaps you want to give them information about how one local church organized its new stewardship campaign. Perhaps you want to entertain them with an account of various mannerisms which may be seen in the pulpit. Perhaps you want to convince them that church membership is an essential aspect of the Christian life. You have some basic idea for a speech.

Not all subjects make good speeches. Some create impossible tasks for both speaker and listener. Others would be a waste of time for all concerned. Before you decide on your subject, evaluate it by asking yourself some of these questions.

1. *What does this subject mean to you?* Are you informed about it? Do you really have a contribution to make to the knowledge or beliefs of your audience? Is any additional information that you might need available to you in the time that remains before you are to speak? How do you feel about the subject? Are you really interested in this area, or are you only

filling time? Do you have a genuine enthusiasm in regard to the importance of this information or the need for the audience to accept the view that you advocate? A salesman will have great difficulty in selling a product unless he is "sold" on it himself.

2. *Is your subject appropriate to the occasion?* Is it too serious when your audience will be in the mood for humor? Is it silly and frivolous in nature when the gathering will be one of serious purpose? Is it suitable to the day, the month, the season of the year? Does it fit the time and place of the meeting?

3. *Does the subject fit the audience?* Can you treat it in such a manner as to suit their intellectual level, their age, their sex? Does the subject have real significance as far as this audience is concerned? The story of your fishing trip last summer probably has no significance to any audience except the members of your immediate family. It would be a poor choice for a speech subject. However, you could utilize the same story to illustrate the importance of preparation before departing on a journey, a subject which is significant to a great many people—all of us who are inclined to be slipshod in making preparation for important future events.

There are at least two pitfalls that speakers should avoid in evaluating their subjects:

1. *Don't worry about the extent of audience interest in your subject.* People are interested in anything and in nothing. The depth of *your* interest is the important consideration. If you are enthusiastic, your enthusiasm can transmit itself to the audience, and they will find themselves becoming interested in spite of themselves. The factor of *significance* concerns your audience; the factor of *interest* concerns you.

2. *Don't confuse the subject itself with your treatment of the subject.* A matter which appears to be serious can be treated in humorous fashion. A clever speaker can bring an erudite subject down to the level of a grade school child. *Alice in Wonderland* appeals to children and still has enough depth for an adult scholar to read it with interest and profit. Sewing may seem an

appropriate subject for ladies and of no particular importance to men. However, many a man has become desperate in his attempts to thread a needle to replace a button on his shirt. A subject may seem impossible for a given audience, but some original treatment of that same subject may make it particularly pertinent. Be sure that your evaluation of any subject includes some consideration of the treatment which you propose to give it.

NARROWING THE SUBJECT

One of the most common mistakes of a beginning speaker (and even of some experienced enough to know better) is to choose a subject that is too broad. Perhaps he is worried about having enough to say to fill the time assigned. As a result, he tries to say everything about everything. Then he either exceeds his time limit, or he bores his audience by repeating the same vague generalizations that they already know. Good speaking always involves novelty in some sense—new information, new relationships, new understandings, new approaches to familiar ideas. Novelty, in turn, requires severe restriction of subject matter, for the new insight can only be appreciated when viewed in the setting of more familiar material. A speaker in any subject area, therefore, has an obligation to use familiar materials in order to educate members of his audience who may not be familiar with his subject, and in order to furnish a background for the real contributions he has to make. He has, moreover, an obligation to be original in some sense, to make a new contribution to the thinking of his audience. He can live up to these two obligations only by staying within a narrow subject area. Thus one of the first jobs in preparing any speech is to narrow the subject.

Several factors will control the amount of limiting that you must do. One, of course, is the time limit of the speech. The shorter the speech, the more you must narrow the subject. A second factor concerns the audience. How much do they know about the subject? If they know very little, you might choose a broader subject and give it a survey treatment, only touching on the important aspects of a broad field. In such a case your main concern will be to limit the subject enough that the sheer mass of information won't confuse the audience. However, if the audience is well informed, you will probably select a narrower subject and treat it more intensively in order to make a real contribution to their understanding. If the audience background in this particular subject area forces you to become more specialized than your own knowledge permits, you had better select another subject before proceeding further. In general, your aim is to tell a lot about a little, not to tell a little about a lot.

Finding the smallest subject area that you plan to discuss is the first step in narrowing your subject. Subjects are like Chinese puzzle boxes; big ones contain a number of small ones, and these in turn contain others smaller yet. The general subject of religion contains smaller subjects, such as Christianity or Buddhism. The subject Christianity, in turn, contains such smaller subjects as Catholicism or Protestantism. The subject of Catholicism would include such smaller areas as the Pope, the Vatican, the Mass. Subject areas can thus be divided into smaller and smaller parts. Your first problem is to narrow your subject to the smallest specific area which will be appropriate to your audience, your time limit, and your purpose in speaking.

Deciding upon the general purpose of your speech is the second step in treating your subject. Three alternatives are open to you. Your speech may be planned to inform, to motivate in some manner, or to entertain. Almost all public address falls into one of these three general classifications. However, certain specific considerations must be kept in mind in regard to these general purposes:

1. *Your decision as to the predominant purpose of the speech*

does not exclude other purposes. Speeches made to motivate should contain solid information. All speeches should be entertaining enough to hold the interest of the audience. Speeches made primarily to inform should also motivate the audience to want the information and to remember it. Nevertheless, you should have one predominant purpose clearly in mind.

2. *The general purpose of motivation is often subdivided into specific types of the change sought:*

To convince—to motivate intellectually.

To persuade—to motivate emotionally.

To activate—to motivate to specific action.

To impress—to motivate by strengthening convictions already present in the listeners' minds.

To stimulate—to motivate in the sense of arousing lofty feelings of patriotism or religious fervor not directly related to a specific point of view.

3. *The speech made solely to entertain should be avoided in this course of study.* Speeches directed at this general purpose are often of unusual types calling for experienced speakers of great skill. Furthermore, the speech to entertain frequently follows the same structures and procedures as the more serious speeches. The speaker who masters the principles of speaking to inform and to motivate, and who is blessed with originality and a sense of humor, should have no great difficulties with the speech to entertain.

Changing your subject into a "topic" is the third step in treating your subject. Note that we are giving a special meaning to this word which is often used interchangeably with "subject." The topic is literally a *topos* or a place where the speech is to be found. Ancient Greek rhetoricians identified specific topics or places where individual arguments could be located—viewpoints from which they could be devised. We use the term with something of the same meaning but with reference to the speech itself rather than to any individual argument.

The "place" where the speech is located is really at the intersection of the subject and the purpose. The subject is that area of human knowledge about which you propose to speak. The general purpose indicates your objective in discussing this area of human knowledge. Combine subject and purpose in a phrase indicative of a specific purpose, and you have a topic. Thus the topic narrows the subject still further and begins to indicate the purpose underlying the speaker's treatment of that subject.

The topic is more than a subject area. It is an aspect of the subject in which intelligent discussion is possible, where varieties of views and opinions might be expressed. On the other hand, the topic is not a proposition that asserts or denies or takes a side. A topic is less than a complete sentence, for a sentence expresses a whole and complete thought while a topic does not. The topic is more open to variety of treatment and interpretation than a sentence would be. The topic is more than just a noun, even a noun that has been modified and restricted by various attached adjectives. The topic is usually expressed in a phrase. It restricts the subject area, but the restriction is in terms of the speaker's general purpose. Here are some examples:

Subject: Christian love
Topic: Developing Christian love in people

Subject: Church attendance
Topic: Reasons for regular church attendance

Notice the difference between a smaller subject area and a topic. A subject, large or small, is simply some area of human knowledge within which a speech could be made. A topic begins to give the speaker's approach to that subject. The fundamental difference between subject and topic, then, is not one of size so much as it is one of purpose. The former indicates nothing of a speaker's purpose at all. The latter begins to hint at what the purpose of the speech will be.

Subject: Education
Smaller subject: Religious education
Topic: Financing your church's program of religious education

In this case, the proposed speech will evidently be informative, giving some methods of financing the program.

Subject: Ethics
Smaller subject: Christian ethics
Topic: Making your personal ethics truly Christian

In this case, the proposed speech will evidently be motivational, seeking to lead its hearers to raise their ethical standards.

As you can see from this discussion, topics may be of several types, depending on the general speech purpose to which they are related. Notice the possible classifications of topics given below:

1. Topics related to the purpose of information
   a. Qualities or attributes of things
      Topic: Qualities of a true Christian
      Topic: The personality of an ideal minister
   b. The nature of things
      Topic: The nature of Christian faith
      Topic: The meaning of the "new birth"
   c. The causes of things
      Topic: The origin of evil
      Topic: Sources of temptation
   d. Kinds of things
      Topic: Types of church music
      Topic: Kinds of denominational structure
   e. Differences or distinctions
      Topic: Differences between Protestants and Catholics
      Topic: Differences between intellectual belief and Christian faith

2. Topics related to the purpose of motivation
   a. Theories

Topic: The substitutionary theory of the atonement
Topic: The premillennial view of the second advent
(Note: The speaker would advocate or oppose the theory mentioned.)

b. Problems
Topic: Solving the problem of division in the church
Topic: Meeting the challenge of secularism

c. Issues
Topic: The Christian view on capital punishment
Topic: The Christian alternative to war

Changing the topic into the purpose sentence of the speech is the final step in narrowing the subject. Various writers speak of this purpose sentence in different terms. Some, particularly the older writers, refer to it as the *proposition*, emphasizing its nature in the speech to convince. Many of the textbooks used in the study of homiletics (the art of preaching) speak of the "proposition of the sermon" in this sense. Other authors, seeking a broader term, call it the *thesis*. We prefer to call it the *central idea* since it is the main idea in the speech from which all other ideas branch and since it serves to give the speech unity.

DEVELOPING THE CENTRAL IDEA

The central idea should have several specific qualities:

1. *It should be a complete sentence, expressing a complete thought.* In this respect it differs from the subject, which is a noun or modified noun, and from the topic, which is a phrase.

2. *It should be single, for its purpose is to insure the unity of the speech.* If the central idea were double, it could not serve in this way.

3. *It should be limited in scope.* The central idea is a promise made to the audience—I intend to discuss this matter. If the area is so large that it cannot be discussed in the available time, the promise must be broken and the audience disappointed. If

you follow the procedure we have outlined of first reducing a subject to the smallest possible area, next reducing that subject area to a topic, and finally reducing that topic to a central idea, you should have no trouble with this requirement.

4. *It should be phrased in such a way as to avoid arousing the prejudices of the audience unnecessarily.* Naturally, the announcement that you propose to argue for a given point of view will produce a certain hostility in the members of the audience who oppose that position. Such hostility is unavoidable, although we shall later discuss some techniques of keeping it to a minimum. If you were to announce, however, that you intend to prove your opponents to be stupid, ignorant fools, you would be arousing hostility unnecessarily.

5. *It should be stated clearly.* Avoid any metaphorical use of language in stating the central idea. Any twist of meaning such as that involved in the use of sarcasm would be out of place. One old saying has it that good speaking is "to tell them what you're going to tell them, tell them, then tell them what you told them." The statement of the central idea should "tell them what you're going to tell them" in the clearest possible manner.

6. *It should express the speaker's purpose, not only in general terms but in terms of this particular speech.* The central idea never conceals the speaker's true objective. If the speaker, for one reason or another, does not want the audience to know his purpose in speaking, he must withhold this thesis until the end; for the minute the audience hear the central idea, they will know his specific purpose.

7. *It should be capable of division.* The central idea looks forward to the rest of the speech and is stated in such a way that the speaker can analyze it, divide it, and treat it section by section. This rule, however, does not apply to all speeches and all central ideas. A few speeches are one-point speeches, with no divisions. In this case, the central idea becomes the only point in the body of the speech. Nevertheless, most speeches have

divisions, and the central idea should be phrased so that it leads smoothly and naturally to such divisions.

The quality of divisibility is extremely important to the central idea since the division process is the next step in speech preparation. After you have phrased the central idea of your speech, you will probably want to divide it into the main sections or "mainheads" of that speech. The wording of the central idea can make this step relatively easy. However, you may also find that the process of analysis and division forces you to rephrase the central idea several times before the speech finally has the structure and unity that you would like. You would be wise, therefore, to give a good deal of attention to the phrasing of the central idea in the first place.

To some extent, the ability of an idea to be divided depends on the complexity of that idea. Such a concept as "the good die young" is difficult to divide. Either it is true or not. As it stands, this idea is not complex enough to provide for much analysis.

Remember, however, that the central idea should also express the speaker's specific purpose. Sometimes a clear grasp of purpose will provide the breaking point which opens the central idea to division. What would be a speaker's purpose in talking to an audience about this idea that the good die young? Perhaps he is speaking upon the occasion of the funeral of a devout youth. His purpose is to point out comforting factors in the situation that exists—the death of a good, young man. The central idea might be stated in terms such as these: "This afternoon I wish to point out why we can find comfort in the tragic death of this young man."

The expression of purpose embodied in the word "why" immediately opens up possibilities for division. We can find comfort because of the quality of the life represented here. We can find comfort because of the promises God has given the righteous. We can find comfort in the resurrection of our Lord.

In order to make the central idea capable of division, therefore, it should include what we might call a "purpose indicator" which will both inform the audience of the speaker's specific purpose and will also lead to the analysis of the central idea. The words which will serve as the basis for this purpose indicator will be words such as "why," "how," "what," and the like.

The beginning speaker should learn to follow a standard form for stating his central idea until such time as the whole concept becomes almost second nature to him. He should make this form the basis for his procedure in planning every speech. When he actually delivers a speech to an audience, however, he can vary the standard form in order to get some variety and even some artistry into his message. At times he may go so far as to use two or three sentences in presenting a single central idea to his audience.

The standard form of the central idea includes three essential parts. These are: (a) transitional elements leading to the statement and calling attention to it; (b) the purpose indicator; (c) reference to the topic. The following examples are typical:

Standard Form (to be used in planning the speech)
  (a) Transitional elements
       "This morning I would like to tell you . . ."
  (b) Purpose indicator
       ". . . why . . ."
  (c) Reference to topic
       ". . . prayer has an important place in the Christian life."
Total central idea in standard form: "This morning I would like to tell you why prayer has an important place in the Christian life."

Varied Form (which might be used in delivering the speech to the actual audience) :
"As Christians you must spend time in prayer, for it is a vital element in the Christian life. Some of you may wonder why I can be so positive about this principle. For a few moments this morning, let me give you the reasons."

Standard Form (to be used in planning the speech)
  (a) Transitional elements
       "Today, I want you to understand . . ."

(b) Purpose indicator
"... how ..."
(c) Reference to topic
"... we can meet the trials of life triumphantly."
Total central idea in standard form: "Today, I want you to understand how we can meet the trials of life triumphantly."

Varied Form (which might be used in delivering the speech to the actual audience):
"The Christian does not escape the times of sorrow and trial in life. His secret is that he overcomes such hours, rather than letting them overcome him. Would you like to live in such a triumphant manner? Let me tell you how."

There is no limit to the possible variations that you might use in stating your central idea to the audience; no limit, that is, except your cleverness and originality. Our main concern, however, must remain with the planning of the speech. In this respect, you will notice the importance of what we have called the purpose indicator. The transitional elements may remain constant, such as: "Today, I would like to tell you." The reference to the topic will always depend on the topic that has been selected. But the purpose indicator will vary with the speaker's purpose in each speech. Notice what these purpose indicators are.

The speech to inform—purpose indicators:
What—when dealing with areas or parts of the topic
How—when dealing with procedures or processes
When—when dealing with time sequences
Who—when dealing with personalities
Where—when dealing with spatial relationships
These purpose indicators may also be coupled with various prepositions to give such combinations as "in what?" "by whom?" "whither?" (to where), and the like.

The speech to motivate—purpose indicators:
Why —when dealing with reasons for the proposed viewpoint or suggested action

What—another possible form for expressing *what* the reasons are.

Some of these purpose indicators are rare. Most speeches will fit into the *what, how,* or *why* classifications.

Be on your guard against certain other words which might, at first glance, appear to be purpose indicators but are not—words which actually block or conceal the expression of the true purpose of your speech. The word "which," for instance, may either help to express the speaker's purpose or may confuse that expression, depending upon how it is used. For instance,

Wrong

"And so we see the two alternatives which confront us. This morning I would like to tell you *which* of these alternatives we should adopt."

In this case, the speaker has concealed his true purpose. He prefers one course of action and intends to argue for it, but his audience, at this point, has no idea of the position he advocates. It may be either of the alternatives. The sentence we have quoted, therefore, cannot be the true central idea of the speech.

Right

"And so you see that I favor the establishment of a family altar in every Christian home. This morning I would like to share with you the reasons *which* have brought me to this position."

In this case, the speaker's purpose is clear; he has stated a true central idea. The word *which* is really a substitute for *what;* he is going to tell *what* the reasons are.

You should be particularly careful of words such as *can, should,* and *would.* These words almost never reveal the speaker's true purpose. Notice the difference between the two central ideas stated below:

Wrong

"Today I would like to discuss the matter of *should* a Christian be expected to tithe."

In addition to the awkward phrasing, this sentence does not make the speaker's purpose clear. Is he in favor of tithing, against it, or is he about to discuss the issues without taking sides?

Right

"Today I would like to discuss the matter of *why* a Christian can be expected to tithe."
Now we know that the speaker favors tithing and that he is about to give us the reasons for his view.

The word "should," like the word "which," may properly appear in the statement of the central idea if the speaker uses it to clarify his intent. For instance, he might announce his purpose in these terms: "Today I would like to tell you *why* a Christian should tithe." In this case, however, the purpose indicator is the word "why"; the word "should" is a part of the reference to the topic.

With all these various considerations in mind, the actual procedure of narrowing a subject to arrive at the central idea of a speech might be as follows:

Subject: Art
Smaller subject: Religious art
Topic: Worship contributions of religious art
Central idea: This evening I want to tell you how religious
   art can make a worship service more meaningful.

Subject: Christianity
Smaller subject: The Lord's Supper
Topic: Significance of the Lord's Supper
Central idea: Let us consider, for a few moments this morn-
            ing, what the true significance of the Lord's Sup-
            per should be for those who partake.

Subject: Christmas
Smaller subject: Christmas gifts
Topic: Making our Christmas giving meaningful

Central idea: I would like to help you understand, in our discussion today, why true Christmas giving requires the giving of one's self.

SELECTING THE TITLE

One other matter remains to be discussed. We have talked about the subject and the topic of the speech in very specific and technical terms, even though these words are often used interchangeably. One other word is sometimes seen in place of subject or topic—the title of the speech. Since we have used subject and topic so technically, we should proceed to give specific meaning to the title, distinguishing it from the subject and the topic.

The title refers to the name that the speaker gives to his speech. It may be defined most easily in terms of its function. It would be used in any preliminary advertising of the speech— "John Jones will speak on (title)." It is also used when the chairman introduces the speaker. The introduction which the audience hears may refer to the subject or topic of the evening's address, but what the chairman actually mentions is the title.

Ministers must give particular attention to their sermon titles. Frequently, the local newspaper expects each preacher to submit the title of Sunday's sermon by noon on Thursday. That title is then announced in the Saturday night edition of the paper. Many churches purchase a newspaper advertisement which announces the title of the forthcoming sermon. Most churches have an outside bulletin board to display sermon titles for the attention of the community. Another common procedure is for the sermon title to be printed in the bulletin or order of worship which members of the congregation have in their hands as they participate in the Sunday morning service. In all of these cases, an effective title can make a real contribution to the sermon by arousing interest and disposing people to listen properly. On the other hand, an ineffective title may be a barrier to attendance and a real handicap to the successful delivery of the sermon.

Since the careful phrasing of the title is so important to every speaker, particularly to the preacher, the following suggestions should receive careful consideration:

1. *Ordinarily, the title should be short and pointed, with real impact.* Such titles as *How to Succeed in Business Without Really Trying* and *How to Become a Bishop Without Being Religious* are exceptions that prove the rule. Both would ordinarily be too long. However, both appeal to basic human motives (success or getting ahead), and both have an unexpected twist. One naturally expects success to be coupled with effort and a bishop to be religious. These titles succeed because they reverse the obvious.

2. *The title should appeal to basic factors of interest in the audience.* "Getting the Most out of Life" would be such a title. Of course, audiences vary. A title like "New Light on Ancient Israel" might have little appeal for the general public but could still be an effective title to use for an address at a convention of scholars.

3. *The title should be related to the subject matter.* In a sense, the title is also a promise of what the speech is to contain. The anticipation raised by the title should not be doomed to disappointment in the speech itself. A sermon entitled "Where Is God?" would have to be more than a theological discussion of the nature of the Trinity. It alludes to the common feeling of alienation from any sense of meaning or purpose in the universe, and the average listener would have a right to expect to receive some practical help in facing this problem. If the preacher offered him none, he would have a right to feel cheated.

4. *The title should not give away the content of the speech.* This rule marks the chief difference between the title and the topic as we have defined it. The topic is too prosaic and too closely related to the speech content. One minister, for example, used "The New Birth" as the subject of a favorite sermon. Then he became aware that this label was, indeed, a subject rather

than a good title. It denoted the subject area treated in the discourse; it offered nothing to arouse curiosity. He finally published the sermon under the heading "The Trouble with Nicodemus," which was a much more effective title. The title should make its reader eager to attend the meeting and to listen to the speech.

5. *The title should be in keeping with the mood of the speech.* If the speech or sermon is to be serious or reverent, the title should not be too light or flippant. One preacher used the title "A Farm, Two Cows, and a Woman" for a sermon based on Luke 14:18-20. The title aroused curiosity, but it was a bit too light for the serious subject of "excuses" discussed in the sermon. Another sermon on Matthew 8:34 was announced by the title "In Love with a Pig." The expression may have been fitting for those ancient people who found their hog business more important than the opportunity to hear Jesus, but it did little to uphold the dignity of the modern pulpit.

Make it your practice to carefully phrase a title for every speech, whether the circumstances require you to state one or not. Be as clever and interesting as you can. Never regard the title as an afterthought to fill the top line of your outline. It is an important part of each speech and can do much toward predisposing the audience in your favor.

Choose your subject carefully; narrow it thoughtfully to an area small enough to be handled; state your specific purpose clearly; give the speech a title which attracts favorable attention —and you are well on your way toward effective speaking.

PROJECTS AND ASSIGNMENTS

Supplementary Reading in the Speech Texts

Baker and Eubanks, *Speech in Personal and Public Affairs,* Ch. 7: Speech and the Pursuit of Ideas; Ch. 8: Major Purposes in Speaking; Ch. 9: Deciding on Subject and Purpose.

Hutchins, ed. *Great Books of the Western World,* Vol. 3, The Great Ideas: II—A Syntopicon of Great Books of the Western World. The section on the "Topic" is found on pp. 1234-38.

Monroe and Ehninger, *Principles and Types of Speech,* Ch. 7: Determining the Subject and the Purpose of a Speech.

Supplementary Reading in the Preaching Texts

Davis, *Design for Preaching,* Ch. 3: Anatomy of the Idea; Ch. 5: What's in a Subject.

Koller, *Expository Preaching without Notes,* Ch. 7: The Homiletical Devices; Ch. 8: The Steps in Preparing an Expository Sermon; Ch. 11: The Heart of the Sermon.

Writing Assignment

Discuss one of the following topics:
1. Choosing a Subject for Platform or Pulpit
2. Purposes and Methods for Narrowing the Subject
3. The Central Idea of the Speech or Sermon
4. The Influence of the Audience on the Selection of the Speech Subject and Purpose
5. The Influence of the Speech Occasion on the Selection of the Subject and Purpose
6. Phrasing an Attractive Title

Speaking Assignment

Prepare and deliver a speech of 3 to 4 minutes in length upon a subject of your own choosing, being sure that the central idea is limited enough for this brief discussion. Prepare an outline for the speech you plan to present. The outline should include the following items, in this order:
1. A title which will arouse interest and attract favorable attention to your speech.
2. The general subject area in which you plan to speak. Be certain this subject is small enough to fit your time limit; use the smallest possible subject.
3. A topic or phrase which further reduces your subject in size and which begins to indicate your general purpose in speaking.

4. A statement of your central idea which clearly indicates, in a single, complete sentence, the point and purpose of this speech.
5. A brief list of the points that you feel you must include in discussing this central idea.

Deliver this speech by stating your central idea and discussing it, being certain to include all of the points which you thought were necessary when you wrote the outline.

Listening Assignment

1. In class, listen carefully to all the other speakers. Take notes by listing the following points for each:
   a. The speaker's name.
   b. The title of the speech and your evaluation of that title.
   c. A statement of the central idea as you understood it.
   d. An evaluation of whether the speaker limited himself to the discussion of this idea or wandered off into other matters.
   e. An evaluation of whether or not the speaker covered this central idea adequately or omitted important areas which he should have included.
2. Outside of class, listen to some other speaker in a formal speech situation (e.g., a minister preaching in a church service, a speaker for a community lecture series, a political speaker on radio or television). Take notes by listing the following points:
   a. The basic facts about this speech: the speaker, audience, occasion, time, place, etc.
   b. A statement of the central idea of this speech as you understand it. (Note: In this case, the central idea will probably not be found first in the speech. In fact, the speaker may state it near the end of the address, or he may only imply it without stating it at all.)
   c. A note as to the point in the speech when the central idea was stated. Was it near the beginning, in the middle, at the end, or merely implied?
   d. Your opinion as to the quality of the discussion of that central idea. Did the speaker limit himself to this central point, or did he wander off on other matters? Did the speaker cover this point adequately?

4

Putting Your Speech in Order

Thus far in our discussion, we have analyzed five aspects of every speech or sermon. Two of these five are parts of the speech itself. The other three are related aspects of speaking. These five parts are:

The parts of the speech itself: (1) the central idea; (2) the discussion of that central idea.

The related aspects: (1) the title—used to attract attention and interest and for the introduction of the speaker by the chairman; (2) the subject—an area of knowledge in which the speech will be prepared; (3) the topic—a more limited area of discussion so phrased as to give the speaker's approach to the subject.

Our consideration of these related aspects now ends. We assume that the student is able to phrase a striking and attractive title and that his skill will grow with further experience. The subject and topic are merely means to an end—that of phrasing a central idea which can both unify the speech and open the way for the discussion and development of subordinate ideas.

Your grasp of the subject and topic will be indicated by the way in which you state the central idea.

The other two parts of the speech now concern us—the central idea and the discussion of that idea. All speeches are made up of these two basic parts. Since these two parts may be presented to the audience in any order, all speeches fall into two general classifications as far as their outline structure is concerned:

1. *The direct order.* The central idea is stated first. The discussion of that idea follows.

2. *The indirect order.* The speech begins with a general discussion of the topic. The central idea follows, as though derived from the discussion that has preceded it.

Since the direct order is obviously the simpler of the two, we shall direct our attention to it first. Some authors refer to this plan of arrangement as "deductive" since it places the general conclusion first and then examines the specific evidence leading to that conclusion. Others refer to this structure as "didactic" since it is the clearest possible way to present ideas to an audience and is particularly useful in teaching. It was this order of speaking which we described in the expression: "First, I tell them what I'm going to tell them. Next, I tell them. Then, I tell them what I told them!"

You will notice that this expression expands our two parts of speech to three parts. Note the development:

1. I tell them what I'm going to tell them—the central idea.

2. I tell them—the discussion of the central idea.

3. I tell them what I told them—a repetition of the central idea which we will call the "conclusion."

You have probably already discovered that it is difficult for a speaker to begin his speech by immediately stating the central idea. Many of the audience would not be prepared to listen at the very beginning of the speech and would thus miss this central point. Such a procedure would also be too abrupt to be artistic. Thus most speakers prepare the audience a bit before they state the central idea in so many words. This process of preparation is called the "introduction," for it serves to introduce people to the central idea and to the discussion which follows.

The direct order, then, includes four major parts of a speech: the introduction, the central idea, the discussion of the central idea, and the conclusion. These four items will vary a great deal in length. Both the introduction and the conclusion will be short, ordinarily. The central idea may be expressed in one sentence. Most of the time consumed by the speech will be spent on the third part, the discussion of the central idea. Hence this part constitutes the bulk or the body of the speech, and writers about public speaking use the terms "body" and "discussion" interchangeably. While these four parts of the speech vary much in length, they are of almost equal importance in their contributions to the effectiveness of the speech.

These four parts constitute the beginning of a plan, blueprint, or outline of the speech. If they are listed in order as the speaker would present them, and if we assign each one its traditional Roman numeral, the list will look something like this:

I. Introduction
II. Central Idea
III. Body
IV. Conclusion

Naturally, the speaker does not *prepare* the parts in this same order. Since the introduction is to introduce the central idea, the speaker cannot prepare it until he has the central idea in mind. By the same token, he cannot prepare the body or discussion of that idea until he has formulated its statement clearly. (In actual practice, many speakers find that the body and central idea grow together as the struggles to develop the discussion of the idea lead to further revisions of the statement of the idea itself.) The conclusion of the speech cannot be prepared until the body has been generally sketched out.

Let us now consider each of these specific parts of the speech in order, so that we can describe them more fully.

THE INTRODUCTION

This part of the speech has two primary functions. It must catch the attention and interest of the audience, and it must introduce the central idea by transmitting that attention naturally and smoothly to the second major part of the speech. In addition, the introduction sometimes serves to provide the audience with background information which may be necessary for grasping and appreciating the speech which follows. On some occasions the speaker may use these opening words to make a courteous response to his introduction or to express his thanks to those who invited him to speak. The two basic functions, however, never vary. The speaker must gain favorable attention, and he must move smoothly into the rest of his speech.

The first sentence is particularly important to the accomplishment of these primary functions. The average person in an audience will listen to a speaker's first few words out of plain curiosity if nothing else. If those words appeal to the basic needs or desires of the members of the audience, those individuals will continue to pay attention. On the other hand, if a speaker's first words are dull, uninteresting, or apologetic, the hearers will quickly turn to other trains of thought that are more appealing. The speaker will be left talking to himself—whether he realizes it or not. If you would be a successful speaker, plan your very first words to capture the interest of the audience.

The second primary function of the introduction also requires careful planning on the part of the speaker. He must see that audience interest is transmitted to the speech itself—that is, to the central idea of the speech. An inexperienced speaker may capture attention with a good joke or story and then lose it again as he changes the subject to get into his real message. The expert speaker plans the introduction to attract attention to the subject area in which the speech will be made, then leads smoothly into a statement of the central idea itself.

These two goals—to interest and to introduce—are obvious.

Any introduction that fails to do both will be a handicap to the speaker and his speech. The techniques which a speaker may use to accomplish these aims are many and varied, limited only by the imagination of the speaker. Consider some of the following possibilities:

1. Ask a series of questions of the audience.
2. Make a reference to the time or occasion.
3. Quote the astonishing words of some other speaker or writer.
4. Tell a dramatic story—or a humorous one.
5. Tell a parable or fable—an "analogy."
6. Make a shocking statement or series of declarations.
7. Refer to what has previously been said or to what has already happened in the meeting. (The necessity of making a response to his introduction may almost force the speaker to use this method.)
8. Refer to some experience that is probably common to most of the members of the audience.
9. Present a conflict, paradox, or contradiction.
10. Use a combination of several of these methods.

Avoid making any abrupt change in the mood of the audience. If they are laughing and unconcerned about serious matters, begin in a light vein and gradually turn their attention to the more serious concerns of your speech. On the other hand, if their mood is sober and grave and your speech is of a serious nature, move into the speech as quickly as you can. Don't break the mood by introducing humor at this point. The effective speaker can sense and adapt to the mood of his audience.

Ministers are among the worst offenders in regard to this matter of beginning a speech in harmony with the mood of the audience. Frequently, a service will have the anthem immediately before the sermon. The choice of the musical selection and the dedicated musicianship of choir and organist may lift the congregation to new spiritual heights. Nothing could be worse than for the preacher to intrude upon such a moment with a stock joke or trivial witticism. In doing so, he is insulting to the musicians and offensive to the congregation. Humor may be a fine method of gaining attention, but it is not a method to be used under these circumstances; it is contrary to the mood of the audience.

The length of the introduction is not as important as its content. It should, nevertheless, be in proportion to the rest of the speech. But the introduction has a job to do. It may supply the audience with background information. It may enable the speaker to respond to the chairman who has just presented him to the audience. It may be used by the speaker to express his thanks to certain individuals or to make preliminary announcements. Whatever else is done, the introduction *must* capture attention and *must* lead into the speech itself. The effective introduction is one which does only those things which need to be done and does them in the briefest and most attractive manner. Begin your speeches in a way that will compel people to listen. Present both yourself and your subject in the most appealing and attractive way that you can. Never apologize. Never break the mood of the audience abruptly. Move to the next section of your speech as quickly as possible.

THE CENTRAL IDEA

This second major part of the speech has already been discussed in some detail. Notice that we have arbitrarily assigned it the second major heading on the outline. In doing so, we have separated it from I, the introduction, and also from III, the body or discussion of the speech. The separation is to remind you that the central idea, while it may be expressed in only one sentence, is just as important to your speech as the introduction, the conclusion, or the body of the speech itself.

This listing of the central idea as a separate part of the outline, distinct from introduction and discussion, results in two outline peculiarities that you should know and understand. First, the second major division on this outline will never have subdivisions. That is to say, division II will never have section A or section B beneath it. The reason is that the divisions of the central idea actually constitute the body of the speech and are thus placed under the third major part of the outline. Note the following examples:

Wrong	*Right*
I. Introduction	I. Introduction
II. Central Idea: _____	II. Central Idea: _____
A. _____	III. Body
B. _____	A. _____
III. Body	B. _____

The second major peculiarity is related to the first. The body will never include a statement of some basic idea which the body then discusses or subdivides. The reason is that such a basic idea has already been expressed on the outline. It is written as the second major part of the speech—the central idea. Compare the following examples:

Wrong	*Right*
I. Introduction	I. Introduction
II. Central Idea: _____	II. Central Idea: _____
III. Body: _____ (a statement of some idea basic to the body)	III. Body
A. _____	A. _____
B. _____	B. _____

In brief, the body of the speech divides and discusses the concept which is written as the central idea. The central idea is the main and basic point which is being discussed in the body of the speech.

THE BODY

The body of the speech, or the discussion, confronts the speaker with a basic choice which has already been mentioned. If the central idea is simple, he may choose not to divide it. In this case, the body of the speech will simply consist of those materials which will serve to make the idea vivid in the minds of the audience. There will be no divisions in this part of the outline. There should be no A, B, C under part III of the outline but only an unnumbered list of the examples and facts which the speaker expects to use in conveying his one idea to his hearers. Such a speech would be a one-point speech, and that one point would be the central idea which has already been expressed as the second major area of the outline.

In most speeches, however, the speaker will turn to a second alternative. He will analyze or divide the central idea into its parts. Then he will consider each of the parts in turn, making it real to the audience. As his hearers grasp each part, they will in turn come to an understanding of the central idea itself. Since this type of structure involves the problems of analysis and division, and since it is the most common type of speech organization, we shall defer the one-point speech for later consideration and deal now with the problems of these divisions or mainheads.

The fact that a speech will have parts or divisions of the central idea in its discussion section will create certain difficulties for you as you plan your speeches. The unity of the speech should be insured by having one central idea. But these divisions constitute additional ideas in the body of the speech. As you move from one idea to the next, you will be in danger of destroying the very unity that you phrased the central idea to insure.

In theory, the problem should not be difficult. You have learned to phrase your central idea carefully, to limit it in size, and to be certain that only one thought is expressed therein. As you proceed to analyze this idea and to develop the mainheads of your speech, you will naturally make all of the subordinate ideas relate to the central idea. Thus the unity of the speech will remain unimpaired.

In actual practice, the procedure is not so simple. One thought leads to another. Ideas must be explained and qualified. Preliminary points intrude as the speaker seeks to prepare his audience for subsequent points. Before long the speech becomes a hodgepodge of ideas that are only related because they all deal with the same general subject matter.

To preserve the unity of your speech, then, the procedure of analysis that you use should keep all the mainheads directly related to the central idea that you are developing. The manner in which you handle words will be particularly important. Ideas cannot be separated from the words which express them. Thus the relationship between ideas will not be clear unless the words which express that relationship are also clear. Such factors of style as parallel construction and the repetition of key words will serve to unify the points in a speech or sermon.

One simple procedure is described below in a series of three steps. You may find the method helpful in the preparation of your speech as you seek to analyze the central idea and determine the subordinate areas which must be included in the discussion in order to make it complete. The device is also useful as a checkup once the speech has been prepared. If you have violated the principle of unity, the location and nature of your error should be obvious. The procedure is as follows:

1. *Make your central idea into a question, using the purpose indicator as the interrogative.* For example:

Central Idea: This morning I would like to help you understand the reasons for the Christian's acceptance of the Lordship of Jesus Christ.
Rephrased as a question: What are the reasons for the Christian's faith in the Lordship of Jesus Christ?

Central Idea: For a few moments, let us examine a simple method which will make our services of worship more meaningful to you.
Rephrased as a question: How can you make the church worship service more meaningful?

You will notice that these questions could actually be those that an interested listener would raise in response to the announcement of the speaker's central idea. The preacher might announce: "This morning I would like to help you understand the reasons for the Christian's acceptance of the Lordship of Jesus Christ."

Then the interested parishioner would respond, in his own mind: "All right, preacher. What are the reasons for our faith in the Lordship of Jesus Christ? Go ahead and tell me."

2. *Make each and every mainhead a direct answer to this question.* For example:

Basic question: What are the reasons for the Christian's faith in the Lordship of Jesus Christ?
Answers: (which are the mainheads)
A. The excellence of Christ's moral character.
B. The spiritual insight of his teaching.
C. The claims he made for himself.
D. The power of his resurrection.

Basic question: How can you make the church worship service more meaningful?
Answers: (which are the mainheads)
A. Make preparation before you come to worship.
B. Understand the meaning of the various aspects of the worship service.
C. Participate completely.
D. Expect something vital to happen.

If the basic question can be regarded as the response of a listener to the announcement of the central idea, then the mainheads represent the speaker's response to the question from the audience. In a church service, the conversation might be somewhat as follows:

Preacher: (aloud) For a few moments, let us examine a simple method which will make our services of worship more meaningful to you.
Listener: (silently) All right, preacher. I've been rather bored with

these services lately. How can I make them more meaningful? Go
ahead and tell me.

Preacher: (aloud) The beginning step in our method is for each worshiper to make the proper preparation before he comes to worship.
Now, by "proper preparation" I mean. . . .

Next, each worshiper must clearly understand the meaning of the
various aspects of our worship service. Take, for instance, the matter of the hymns. . . .

And so the preacher will continue through the other mainheads
in that elaboration which constitutes the body of his sermon.

Notice the perfect relationship between the wording of the
central idea and the wording of each mainhead. The central
idea promises that the speaker will tell his audience *why* he
supports a given position. His mainheads give his reasons *why.*
Or his central idea may promise information about *how* a certain process is carried out. Then the mainheads must consist of
steps *how.* If the central idea promises to tell *what* areas of a
particular topic are significant, the mainheads must reveal *what*
those areas are. Even minor flaws in wording will spoil the unity
and logic of the speech. For instance,

Wrong

Central Idea: This evening I want to make clear for every caller the
steps that you will follow in helping with our annual stewardship
campaign.

Body:

A. You will be given a packet of the material you need.

Notice that this mainhead is not a "step." It indicates something done for the caller rather than something done by the
caller, an action he receives rather than an action he initiates.
The speaker has a proper subordinate area in mind for his mainhead, but the wording really doesn't make sense. Imagine how
a conversation between speaker and listener would sound in
this case.

Speaker: (aloud) This evening I want to make clear for every caller the steps that you will follow in helping with our annual stewardship campaign.

Listener: (silently) Very good! I'm eager to help. What is the first step you want me to take?

Speaker: (aloud) First, you will be given a packet of the material you will need.

Listener: (silently and impatiently) That's all very well, and I'm glad to know somebody will be doing something. But what do you want me to do? What is the first step you want me to take?

The same mainhead can easily be revised to fit the wording of the central idea:

Right

Central Idea: This evening I want to make clear for every caller the steps that you will follow in helping with our annual stewardship campaign.

Body:

A. You should first become familiar with the materials that you will be using.

Now the mainhead is a step, indicating the first thing that the caller is expected to do. The wording makes sense, and the listener is satisfied that he is receiving clear and logical instruction. The procedures will be better fixed in his memory, and his confidence in the speaker will be increased. Never be satisfied with your outline until central idea and mainheads are in perfect agreement. Revise either the central idea or each mainhead statement until you are certain they all fit together.

3. *Be sure that all the mainheads answer the basic question in the same way.* In other words, make sure that all utilize the same principle of division. Violation of this rule will usually result in a loss of unity or an overlapping of mainheads. Study the following examples:

Wrong

Basic question: What are the disadvantages of marrying outside of one's faith?

Answers: A. Religious differences may raise psychological barriers.

B. Religious differences may cause conflicts of conscience.

C. Different group affiliations may cause social frictions.

D. Difficulties may be multiplied by the problems of rearing the children.

Notice that mainhead D introduces a chronological element that is missing in A, B, and C. These first three answers deal with topics or areas of difficulty—psychological, ethical, and social problems. The last answer does not specify the nature of the "difficulties" in this manner but predicts they will increase after children are born. Thus D may overlap A, B, and C since difficulties following the birth of children will probably continue to be psychological, ethical, or social in nature. In sum, the speaker who prepared this outline shifted his principle of division between C and D. His first three answers follow a topical system of division; the fourth switches to a chronological system.

In this case, the error should not be difficult to correct. The speaker could change his outline to read:

Right

Basic question: What are the disadvantages of marrying outside one's faith?

Answers: A. Difficulties in the husband-wife relationship

1. Psychological conflicts
2. Ethical conflicts

B. Difficulties in the total family relationship

1. Conflicts relating to the children
2. Conflicts relating to in-laws
3. Conflicts relating to the rest of society

This outline follows the same principle of division in creating its two mainheads. The subheads under A differ a bit since they begin to touch on the causes of conflict rather than just the areas in which conflict occurs. However, both subheads follow the same principle of division. The outline is now correct.

Naturally, the body of the speech includes more than these points and sub-points. The speaker must discuss these matters with his audience. Later, we shall give more attention to the techniques that he uses. For the present, we may regard the speaker as fulfilling his obligation if he states each point, explains exactly what he means, and then refers to a case—some event that actually happened or which could have happened—which demonstrates how this principle works or what it really means. For instance, the speaker pointing out ethical conflicts in a mixed marriage might tell of one particular couple who separated because the wife refused to cook roast beef on Friday and the husband didn't like fish.

The body of every speech consists of two different elements. One of these elements is the idea structure, the points of the speech, the mainheads and subheads. The other consists of the materials used by the speaker to get these points across to his audience. This difference between ideas and materials is basic, and you should be certain that you have it clearly in mind.

Perhaps you can understand the difference better if you trace the choices that any speaker has in preparing to develop the central idea of a speech. Suppose that he has phrased his central idea and is now ready to develop it.

Decision one (which must be made about the central idea) :

1. He can decide that his central idea is simple; he needs only to add materials to make it vivid for the audience. In this case, the body of the speech will have no divisions or mainheads. It will consist of the explanation and illustration of the single point which is the central idea. His speech will be a one-point speech.

2. Or he can decide that his central idea must be divided into subordinate areas, into ideas which will be the mainheads or main divisions of the speech. If he makes this decision and formulates the mainheads, he is ready for . . .

Decision two (which must be made about every mainhead):

1. He can decide that his mainhead is simple, that he needs only to add materials to make it vivid for the audience.

2. Or he can decide that his mainhead must be divided into subheads or subordinate divisions of the mainhead. The principles that he would follow in dividing the mainhead are the same as those used in dividing the central idea. If he makes this decision and formulates the subheads, he is ready for . . .

Decision three (which must be made for every subhead):

1. He can decide that his subhead is simple, that he needs only to add materials to make it vivid for the audience.

2. Or he can decide that the subhead must be divided into further subordinate divisions. If he makes this decision and formulates sub-subheads, he is ready for . . .

Decision four—and so on.

Obviously, the speaker soon reaches a situation where he has all ideas and no speech, where he has so much structure that neither he nor his audience can remember the points. The important thing to remember is this: Analyze as you will, you eventually reach the point where you must take the first alternative. Your smallest idea must be made vivid to the audience by the use of speech materials—these explanations and stories we have been discussing. Then if the audience grasps the subordinate ideas, they will grasp the main ideas which are being developed. If the audience grasps the main ideas, they will then grasp the central idea of the speech.

These two basic things—the ideas or thought structure, and the speech materials—make up the body of the speech. The thought structure is speaker-oriented, pointing to the central idea and to your basic purpose in making the speech. The materials are audience-oriented, bridging gaps of unconcern or of misunderstanding so that your ideas and feelings are accurately communicated to the minds of your listeners. Together, they constitute your discussion of the subject you set out to discuss.

THE CONCLUSION

The final section of the speech is to conclude it, a fact which some speakers never learn. The conclusion should round out the thought and make the speech seem finished. It is never merely a tail attached to the last mainhead; it should conclude the speech as a whole. It should leave the central idea fresh in the minds of the audience. On some occasions the conclusion may be used to move the audience to adopt a particular viewpoint or to begin a specific program of activity. It should constitute the emotional high point of the speech. On the other hand, it should not become a separate speech in its own right, nor should it open up some new area for consideration.

Specific methods for finishing the speech and for accomplishing the various other functions which a conclusion may serve are almost unlimited. Some of the common ones are:

1. Summarize by repeating the central idea and mainheads. This is a very common method, especially in the speech which is planned to inform.

2. Use a story or analogy. The Sermon on the Mount ends in this fashion (Matt. 7:24-27). Some speakers like to begin a story in the introduction, telling just enough to arouse curiosity and lead into the central idea, and then finish the same story for the conclusion.

3. Use a quotation from some other speaker or writer. Here is a wonderful opportunity to use that verse of poetry which expresses so well what you are trying to say in this speech.

4. Refer to an idea or statement which was used in the introduction. This technique is especially useful to give that "finished" feeling to the speech.

5. Give the specific steps of the action you want your listeners to take. (Remember, however, that you are not to begin on a new speech.)

6. Answer the question "so what?" about your speech.

Like the introduction, the conclusion should never be weak,

uncertain, or apologetic. Avoid the words "in conclusion." If the speech is well organized, the audience will recognize the conclusion without your telling them, and the label will only break the flow of thought. If you have really arrived at the conclusion, end the speech without making the announcement. If you have not arrived at the conclusion, don't make a promise you do not intend to fulfill.

Keep the conclusion moving. The audience has just listened to a whole speech, and many are impatient for the end. Don't keep them waiting any longer than is necessary to accomplish your purpose. You may summarize, but don't give the speech over again. Bear in mind the old rule for a successful speech: "Be interesting, be brief, be seated."

The words "thank you" at the end of the speech are also unnecessary. The audience should thank you for a good speech well delivered. You have done the real work.

These four parts—introduction, central idea, body, and conclusion—constitute the major sections of most speeches. Under certain circumstances, if you know what you are doing, you may omit some of these parts or change their order. For the present, however, try to be as effective as you can in following these four steps:

1. Capture their attention and interest.
2. Tell them what you're going to tell them.
3. Tell them.
4. Tell them what you told them.

PROJECTS AND ASSIGNMENTS

Supplementary Reading in the Speech Texts

Brigance, *Speech: Its Techniques and Disciplines in a Free Society,* Ch. 11: Organizing the Speech; Ch. 12: Beginning and Ending the Speech.

Gray and Braden, *Public Speaking: Principles and Practice,* Ch. 14:

Outlining and Planning; Ch. 15: Introducing the Speech; Ch. 16: Concluding the Speech.

White, *Practical Public Speaking,* Ch. 5: Organizing the Body of the Speech; Ch. 8: Developing the Introduction of the Speech; Ch. 9: Developing the Conclusion of the Speech.

Supplementary Reading in the Preaching Texts

Blackwood, *The Preparation of Sermons,* Ch. 10: The Art of the Introduction; Ch. 11: The Concern about Structure; Ch. 14: The Force of the Conclusion.

Jones, *Principles and Practice of Preaching,* Ch. 5: Outlining the Sermon: General Principles and Procedures; Ch. 9: Preparing the Introduction and Conclusion.

Knott, *How to Prepare a Sermon,* Ch. 5: The Introduction; Ch. 6: The Main Divisions; Ch. 8: The Conclusion

Writing Assignment

Discuss one of the following topics:
1. The Outline: Help or Hindrance?
2. The Purpose and Plan of the Introduction
3. The Art of Concluding a Speech
4. Beginning and Ending the Sermon
5. Maintaining the Unity of the Sermon
6. The Sermon Outline: Its Nature, Form, and Purpose

Speaking Assignment

Prepare and deliver a speech of 4 or 5 minutes in length on a subject of your own choosing. Prepare an outline according to the following pattern for the speech you plan to present:

Title: ————————————

I. Introduction
   Method to be used: ———————————————

II. Central Idea: ——————————————————

III. Body
    Mainhead A _____
        Material to be used: _____

    Mainhead B _____
        Material to be used: _____

    Mainhead C _____
        (You will have at least two mainheads and not more than
        about five. Outline them all in a similar manner.)

IV. Conclusion
    Method to be used: _____

Deliver this speech in such a way that the parts will stand out clearly
for your audience.

Listening Assignment

1. In class, listen carefully to all the other speakers. List the following
   points for each:
   a. An evaluation of the introduction from the standpoint of audi-
      ence interest. Did it capture and hold the attention of the
      audience?
   b. The statement of the central idea as you understood it.
   c. The statement of each mainhead.
2. Outside of class, listen to some other speaker in a formal speech
   situation. List the following points:
   a. The basic facts about this speech: speaker, audience, occasion,
      time, place, etc.
   b. An evaluation of the introduction from the standpoint of audi-
      ence interest.
   c. The statement of the speaker's central idea as you understood
      it. Was it stated or implied? At what point in the speech was
      the central idea stated?
   d. The statement of each mainhead, if the speaker had divisions
      in this speech.
   e. The technique used for the conclusion.

5

Keeping It Clear for
Your Audience

You have now learned to express your ideas under the discipline
of the parts of a formal speech. You have caught the attention of
the audience with an introduction, expressed your chief point as
a central idea, made that point vivid for the audience as you
analyzed it into mainheads and discussed them, and left a lasting
impression with the conclusion. These parts of the speech, however, may have caused some new problems for you as a speaker.
For one thing, the increase in the number of parts and divisions
will naturally multiply the chances for confusion on the part
of your audience. Also, it creates a new problem for you as the
speaker—the problem of moving from one of these sections to
another. Good speaking does not leave the audience in a state
of confusion; neither is it jerky and disjointed. The speech
should move with a certain flow from one section to another; yet,
it should not become so smooth and artistic that the listeners
become lost.

TRANSITIONS

One of the difficulties in speaking centers at the "joints" of the speech, those gaps where one part or idea ends and the next begins. The transition or bridge at each of these spots should be phrased in such a manner that the speech flows smoothly from one section to another. In addition, the speaker should utilize these transitions to orient the audience to where he has been, where he is, and where he is going.

You must understand that listeners are not readers, that a speaker is not a writer, and that a speech is not a composition which is being delivered orally. In fact, we could make a good case for the opposite of each of these ideas. A writer is primarily a speaker who happens to put his ideas on paper; a reader listens with his eyes; and a composition is simply a speech frozen in print. A genuine speech is an encounter between living people— a speaker and his audience—meeting upon some specific occasion to think together around some topic of the speaker's choosing. What goes on between speaker and audience is a dialogue, with the speaker talking and the audience answering by the thousand little signs that an alert speaker will notice and to which he will respond. In this constantly fluctuating interchange, some fixed points and some guideposts are necessary. The introduction, central idea, mainheads, and conclusion will provide the settled areas to be explored. The transitions are the guideposts, pointing from one idea to the next, so that both speaker and audience may be reminded of precisely where they are.

This fluid nature of oral communication makes careful transitions far more important in speaking than in writing. Transitions in a speech will be longer; they may on some occasions attain considerable length. This difference is only reasonable. If a reader becomes lost during the interchange of ideas between himself and the writer, he need only look back in order to remind himself of the subject of the discussion and to reorient himself. But if the hearer becomes lost in the more fluid speech situation, what is he to do? Can he raise his hand and ask for a review of the last three points? Few listeners have the courage to do so, even in a college lecture class where questions are encouraged. Thus the speaker who cares anything at all about holding his audience may need to spend an entire paragraph of his address in orienting them before he moves to a new idea. The writer needs to provide only a few words or a phrase of transition in order to move smoothly to his next point.

Coupled with these various considerations is the matter of the fluctuating attention of the audience. They are human beings, not recording machines. A man cannot fix his attention on any one thing for more than a few seconds at a time. Concentrate as he will, his attention will shift in spite of his best efforts. The attention of any audience is in a constant flux, moving to the speaker and his words, then away to a tremendous range of other things, then (perhaps) back to the speaker and his speech. If you could take an "attention cross section" of your audience at any particular instant during any one of your speeches, you might find a few actually listening to your words. Most of them would be concentrating, for that instant, on almost everything else you could imagine.

At those moments in your speech when you are telling an interesting story, the shifting attention of the audience need not concern you. Each individual may miss a few of the details of your story, but all of them will catch enough to comprehend the general flow of the narrative. Besides, the story probably has some dramatic value in itself. The attention of the listener may wander; but it will not wander far, and it will soon come back to the story.

However, other parts of the speech, such as the central idea and the main divisions, have less entertainment to offer. These parts are crucial; if the audience should miss them, you may be frustrated in your purpose in delivering the entire speech. What if the audience happens to be giving attention to other matters when these important concepts are stated?

Let us take an attention cross section of your audience at the point when you state your central idea. At that instant you have done everything you could to draw the attention of the audience and to fasten it upon your words. You planned your introduction to arouse interest and to point to that central idea. Now the very manner in which you speak changes as you announce the central idea with all the force and emphasis of which you are capable. You may even gesture with the fist or index finger to attract attention to your words. In response to these factors, most of the members of your audience are probably listening. But be realistic; people are human, and no speaker has achieved perfection. A few members of your audience are thinking of other things rather than listening to you. These people miss your central idea, and for them the rest of the speech is largely wasted.

The problem does not end at this point but continues to multiply throughout the rest of the speech. As each of your subsequent points is stated, additional members of the audience are lost. They happen not to be listening when you express each mainhead, and the rest of the speech becomes a mystery to them. By the time you finish, a large portion of the audience may have not the faintest idea of what you have been talking about.

The problem of the lost and confused audience thus springs from many causes—from the complexity of the speech, from the fluid nature of the speaking situation, and from fluctuating attention. The solution to the problem is up to you as the speaker. You will want to keep the interest level of your speech high, not only in the introduction but in the rest of the speech as well. You will want your voice and gestures to be lively and attractive. Above all, you will want to provide those frequent reviews and internal summaries which constitute speech transitions.

A transition may be defined as an internal summary. It repeats the significant points that have gone before, ties them together, and links them to the next idea that is to come. In this manner it informs the audience precisely where the speaker has been, where he is, and where he is going. The constant repetition required for the transition serves to remind the audience of points heard earlier and forgotten, and in the repetition some listeners may hear points that were missed entirely when first stated.

The process of making a transition may be outlined as follows:

1. *Repeat all significant ideas previously developed.* The key word here is "significant." Naturally, the idea which you have just been discussing is significant; repeat it. Other ideas which correlate with this one are also significant and should be repeated. That is to say, if your last idea was a mainhead, repeat all the earlier mainheads. If your last idea was a subdivision, repeat all the earlier subdivisions. If your ideas are really very simple, if they have been repeated a number of times already, or if your audience has some visual reminder such as a chart or model, you may be safe in omitting some of the earlier points. Be careful, however; it is better to repeat too much than too little. Repeat the idea which you are finishing in any case.

2. *Remind the audience of the unity of these ideas by showing their relationship to each other.* You show this relationship by repeating the idea which ties all the others together. If you are dealing with mainheads, repeat the central idea that unites them. If you are dealing with subdivisions, repeat the main division that unites them. If you are moving from a final subhead to the next mainhead, tie the earlier subheads together by repeating the mainhead; then go back and repeat the central idea so that the mainheads will be united also.

3. *State the next idea in sequence in the speech.* The transition is a bridge by which one moves from one idea to the next. The repetition of the previous idea constitutes one abutment of the bridge. Your indication of the unity of these ideas makes the body of the bridge. You build the other abutment of the bridge by stating the new idea which you are about to develop.

Perhaps we can explain the procedure more clearly if we imagine a speech situation and think of what the speaker might say in following each of these three steps. Suppose that the outline looks something like this:

II. Central Idea: This morning I wish to explain how you can find God for yourself.
III. Body
    A. Be sure you're looking for the right God.
    B. Look for him in the right place.

The speaker has finished his discussion of the first mainhead and is ready to move to the second. What would he say in order to make this transition?

Step 1—Repeat. Only two significant ideas have been presented earlier in this speech, the central idea and the first mainhead. The central idea will be repeated in step 2, so the speaker need not repeat it here. He will thus repeat only the first mainhead: "Those who would find God, then, must be certain that they look for the right God. . . ."

Step 2—Remind. The speaker is moving from one mainhead to the next. In order to remind the audience of the unity of the mainheads, he must naturally refer to the central idea. His repetition of this thesis will constitute the second step in the transition: "In addition, if you would know God for yourself . . ."

Step 3—Move ahead. Now the speaker is ready to state his second mainhead: ". . . you must look for him in the right place."

The complete transition could be made in these words: "Those who would find God, then, must be certain that they look for the right God. In addition, if you would know God for yourself, you must look for him in the right place."

Be very careful in following this procedure, however; it can easily become mechanical and inartistic. Introduce variety in every way that you can. Nothing is sacred about the order of these three steps. Try them in various ways, even within the course of one speech. Vary the wording and the sentence structure as much as you can. At times, you may want to introduce numbers—"first, second, third." At other times numbers become too obvious and crude; leave them out.

Perhaps we can see some of the possibilities for variation by looking once more at our speech giving instructions for finding God. The speaker has moved ahead through the discussion of three mainheads. He is ready, now, to move into the fourth. His transition might sound something like this: "And so we continue our quest for God. We have done our best to rid ourselves of misconceptions and to look for the right God. We have tried to see beyond the physical universe that we might look in the right place. We have examined and clarified our motives. May we now be certain of finding him? The answer must still be 'no' until we have satisfied one further requirement. We must follow proper procedures in our search; we must look for God in the right way."

In this case the unity of ideas is indicated by references to the central idea at the beginning and near the end. The repetition of previous significant ideas takes place in the middle with the three earlier mainheads being repeated in normal order. Finally, the speaker moves to his fourth mainhead which he is about to discuss. He has introduced some variety into the procedure, but his summary is so clear that a hearer could reconstruct the outline from this paragraph alone.

When is a transition needed? Some sort of bridge or internal summary is necessary whenever the speaker shifts from one point to the next. If these points are minor, the summary may be brief, the review less than complete. Subheads might be related to one another and to the mainhead without mention of the central idea. But whether the new point that the speaker intends to add is a major one or a minor one, some type of summary-transition will be necessary.

This principle holds for the ideas of the speech, not for the developmental materials. The speaker may add another story or a further explanation without a major review. He may use words such as, "Or take the recent case of . . ." or "In addition, you should remember that . . ." Such expressions will be quite enough as a rule. If the material he is presenting is detailed and extensive, he will probably repeat the mainhead several times in the course of the discussion, but ordinarily he will present no other ideas than the one he is trying to develop. The full summary-transition will wait until he is ready to move to his next idea.

The techniques that we have suggested break down at one point—when the speaker moves from the introduction of the speech to the statement of his central idea. So far, no significant ideas have been advanced, and no principle of unity has yet been stated. Our usual bridge here could have only one abutment, the abutment resting on the central idea itself. To overcome this difficulty, most speakers make some reference to the time, the occasion, or the speaker's purpose in phrasing the transition. In chapter 3 we called these devices the "transitional elements" of the central idea. You may think of them as part of the central idea or as the transition which bridges from introduction to central idea. In either case they close the gap and center the attention of the audience upon the speaker's basic point which follows.

The following example should help you understand the points at which a transition is needed and the basic procedures to be followed in phrasing it. With a little originality, you can make the transitions in your speeches much more artistic and appealing.

I. Introduction
   Transition: Since you are interested in the possible choice of the ministry as a vocation . . .
II. Central Idea: I want to point out to you this evening what the basic requirements for a properly prepared minister are.
   Transition: The first, though not necessarily the most important of these requirements is . . .

III. Body

    A. The minister must be an educated man.

        Transition: Certainly, none of us would deny the importance of education in this broad sense. We would make a mistake, however, if we considered learning the only requirement for the clergyman. His work also involves certain professional skills, and thus . . .

    B. The minister must be a skillful man.

        Transition: These specific skills, however, and even the minister's general education are not truly basic. Even the most unprepared individual could probably learn enough from schooling and experience to serve as a helpful pastor. One further area remains, a requirement which is primary and more important than any other. Above all,

    C. The minister must be a good man.

        Transition: The term "good" wins our approval, but it is almost empty of specific meaning. In order to understand it, let us examine three specific aspects of "goodness" which the pastor should exhibit. First,

        1. He should embody the highest ethical and moral standards.

            Transition: The minister's ethics, as we have described them, constitute the negative aspect of his goodness. In addition to being a good man in this sense,

        2. He should be a kindly man.

            Transition: Goodness, then, means a moral uprightness which does not become puritanical. The minister displays the highest ethical standards in his conduct, but he tempers righteousness with human kindness in dealing with his fellow men and women. In so doing, he begins to approach the third and ultimate aspect of goodness,

        3. He should be a Christlike man.

            Transition: When we say that the minister is good, then, we mean that he is morally upright in his conduct, that he is kindly in his relations with others, and that he does his best to follow the example of Christ in all things. Thus he meets the third of the basic requirements for the properly prepared minister. He is an educated man, a skillful man, and, above all, a good man.

IV. Conclusion

Notice the manner in which the various transitions follow the standard pattern. Significant earlier ideas are repeated. These are constantly united with the central idea so that their unity is obvious. The wording varies, but the ideas are repeated over and over. Each transition serves as a bridge to reach the next point in the speech.

One further comment is necessary in regard to the conclusion. In the sample outline given, the conclusion would not consist of a simple summary. If it did, the transition from the last subhead into the conclusion would be much reduced; the summary conclusion would provide the necessary review. In the example above, the transition provides the review, and the speaker would use a story, a quotation, or some other method of concluding the address.

THE DELIVERY

If the speech has been carefully and logically constructed and if the transitions are properly made, there is no reason why its content should confuse or mislead its hearers. Unfortunately, the listener does not hear a speech; he hears a speaker. The content cannot be separated from the delivery. As we said earlier, a speech is an encounter between living people. A speaker must phrase his ideas and repeat them in order to adapt to the realities of the attention span of his audience. In like manner he should control the sound of his voice and the movements of his body in such a way that he will command attention and will focus that attention upon the basic ideas he wishes to convey.

In other words, your physical presence in front of the audience, as well as the content of the speech, must reach out to seize and hold the attention of every individual. Your appearance and the sound of your voice as you stand before those people must serve to make contact between your ideas and the minds of the group.

Their attention may fluctuate, but you should speak in such a manner that their thoughts can never rest for long on anything else.

If you will remember the various speakers you have heard, you will recognize that the manner of speaking vitally affects the ideas being expressed. A speaker can talk in such a way as to enhance the ideas, adding interest that the ideas alone do not have, clarifying the structure and purpose of the speech, and impressing the ideas on the memory of his hearers. On the other hand, a speaker may deliver his speech in such a manner that he confuses the listener, contradicts the thoughts which he is expressing, and creates in the minds of some of his audience a negative emotional reaction which may spread to include the subject matter of the speech and the very personality of the speaker.

That aspect of speaking which confronts the audience and commands their attention is called "audience contact." It springs from the speaker's sincerity and from the intensity of his desire to communicate his message to his hearers. It includes several important factors which you should consider as you work to make yourself a more vital and interesting speaker.

Contact the audience with your mind. Make your speech a genuine experience of communication, a circular interchange with the listeners. As you talk, part of your mind will be on your words, thinking of the next idea and the manner in which you plan to express it. But another part of your consciousness should be engaged in the receiving aspect of the conversation with your audience. They will be answering you throughout the speech with a thousand little movements and signs. Train yourself to notice these indications and to adapt your speech to them.

A yawn may tip you off that the speech is getting dull—make the next story a bit more dramatic. Or the members of the audience may be inspecting their watches—get to the conclusion as quickly as possible. Frowns may indicate that your point wasn't understood—go over the explanation again, a little more clearly this time. A strained look may indicate that the person can't hear you—speak up! Be alert and responsive to the speech that the audience makes to you.

Contact the audience with your eyes. We don't trust a shifty-eyed person. We recognize that when little Johnnie has been stealing jam, he hates to look mamma in the eye. The individual who constantly stares at his feet is usually regarded as bashful. If you want to look guilty, bashful, or weak, just neglect to look at your audience. On the other hand, if you want to appear confident, powerful, dynamic, and straightforward, look them in the eye.

Never stare at one person long enough to embarrass him. Look at one for only a few seconds before shifting your gaze to someone else. Include all parts of the audience from time to time. But never look above the heads of your audience, in front of them, or to the right or left of them unless you have some good reason for doing so.

Be particularly careful to maintain eye contact at any time when something happens to distract attention. If some noise comes from outside, for instance, don't call attention to the disturbance by looking at it. Concentrate every effort on looking at the audience and keeping their attention centered on you. Beware of the surreptitious glance at your watch which not only breaks eye contact but makes the audience time-conscious. Train yourself to speak without notes so that you need not look away from the audience in order to refresh your memory. Contact the audience constantly with your eyes.

Contact the audience with your voice. There are four basic ways to accomplish this:

1. *Be heard.* You will have difficulty establishing any sort of contact with your audience unless they can hear you. Speak up! Imagine a particularly difficult person standing at the very back of the room, an individual who is both hard of hearing and in-

tellectually obtuse. Speak loudly enough, clearly enough, and simply enough that such a person cannot miss or misunderstand your ideas.

Worry seldom helps in the delivery of a speech. If you become concerned about what to do with your hands, how you look, how you stand, how you pronounce words, or about the quality of your grammar, the worry will only make you self-conscious and more prone to error. If you must worry, then worry about someone's missing a word. If you must be afraid, be afraid that someone might have to strain to hear what you are saying.

2. *Be understood.* Volume alone is not enough. If the audience hears only the drone of your voice, they will first feel frustrated, then sleepy. You should pronounce each vowel and consonant so that it is quite distinct from the other sounds of the language. "Sat" and "set" are not the same word, even though the consonants are identical; one may not be substituted for the other without serious grammatical consequences. "Weather" and "whether" are distinguished only by the sounds that begin the words, and the difference between these two "w" sounds is very slight. Be sure the audience doesn't have to depend on the context to know which word you are using. Pay particular attention to final consonant sounds. Don't substitute one sound for another as in saying "fishin" and "huntin" in place of "fishing" and "hunting." You should neither omit the final sound nor overemphasize it by adding an "uh" at the end as some speakers do:

Wrong	*Right*	*Wrong*
chursh	church	church-uh
Biboo	Bible	Bible-uh
Chris'	Christ	Christ-uh

Many speakers have become famous and have been very effective on the platform or from the pulpit in spite of poor grammar or foreign accents, but they never did so by talking as though their mouths were full of mush. Even a whisper, if carefully articulated, may be heard to the farthest corner of a large auditorium. Shouting, without care in articulation, will wear out your voice while communicating nothing of your message. Speak clearly.

3. *Be conversational.* Think of your speech as no more than an enlarged conversation. Be certain that you are heard and understood, but don't adopt the mannerisms of the soapbox orator. Your purpose is to communicate ideas, not to put on a show. You will speak a bit more slowly and distinctly to match the larger setting in which you speak, but the basic pattern of your delivery should remain that of direct conversation.

4. *Be pleasant.* Few speeches are so serious in nature that they can't be started with a smile. Keep that same friendly smile in your voice all of the way through the talk. Avoid the sneer or the sarcastic sound. Some speakers have trouble with voices that are harsh, hoarse, or nasal. While some of these problems may call for the services of a professional speech clinician, most of them can be helped by easy, relaxed voice production. Think of yourself as a friendly person sharing his ideas with a group of those whom he knows and loves. Let this attitude show in your voice and in all aspects of your speech delivery.

Contact the audience with your hands. One of the first rules of camouflage is that anything that appears out of place will be noticed. Your hands will not be noticed as you speak if you leave them in a normal position—resting quietly on the stand before you, hanging at your sides, or any other place that seems natural for you. In most cases, they will then look perfectly natural to the audience. Concentrate on your speech. If you become conscious of your hands, your audience will too, and their attention will be diverted from your message.

Frequently, beginning speakers will attempt to hide their hands, perhaps in a pocket, behind their back, or clasped in front. Remember that any of these positions could move the hands from their normal spot and thus call attention to them.

At times, however, you will want the audience to notice your hands because you are using them in some manner to add to the total effect of the speech. For instance, you may want to point to some object as you mention it. Then put the hands in motion, take them out of the normal position, and the audience will notice the movement and follow it toward the object you want them to see. They will not be aware of the gesture as such, but your hands will have made their contribution to the total pattern of communication.

The habit of talking with your hands is not some peculiar or unnatural procedure, even though it may be the subject of many jokes. Watch those around you as they forget themselves in their involvement in everyday conversation. See how active their hands become. The same type of uninhibited expression, natural and relaxed, should characterize your platform delivery. Don't be afraid to contact the audience with your hands.

Contact the audience with your feet. The way you walk and the way you stand will affect your audience contact. The following suggestions may help you:

1. *"Lean into" the audience.* Keep your weight forward, on the balls of your feet. If you are standing with one foot in front of the other, keep your weight either equally divided or on the forward foot. Putting the weight on the rear foot makes you appear sloppy and relaxed, and your audience may begin to feel that way too. Stand as if you are alive and awake, with something to say and eager to say it.

2. *"Walk into" the audience.* If you want to move around during your speech (and you should), remember that a speaker has four general directions in which he can walk. One is to take a few short steps directly forward toward the audience. A second is to take a step or two directly back away from the audience. The third is to move at an angle toward the corner of the audience on the left, and the fourth is to move at an angle toward the corner of the audience on the right. Except for the short backward movement, you will always be walking into the audi-

ence. If you possibly can, avoid moving to one side or the other by walking parallel to the front of the audience. Move forward, directly or at an angle, by walking toward a section of the audience, speaking directly to that section toward which you are walking, and thinking: "Here's an important part of my speech. I want *you* particularly to understand it. These remarks are directed straight at *you*."

3. *Move to fit the scene.* Remember that the audience sees you as one part of a total scene or picture. The front of the auditorium, classroom, or sanctuary constitutes the frame in which you are placed. Everything that the members of the audience can see as they watch you will also be a part of the same picture. This scene must be reasonably harmonious, or people will begin to think that something is wrong. If the setting in which you speak is narrow and restricted, your movements must be carefully controlled and confined, or you will appear to be an overexuberant and effusive speaker. On the other hand, the wide stage of some huge auditorium calls for proportionately large gestures and movements, or you may appear to be shy and self-conscious.

Establish the contact. The speaker should contact the audience with his mind, his eyes, his hands, and his feet before he ever makes a sound with his voice. Remember that your speech begins at the moment that you first receive the attention of the audience. On some occasions it may begin before you can move a muscle. The chairman finishes his introduction, announces your name and the title of your speech, turns, nods in your direction, and resumes his seat. The audience turns toward you, eager to hear what you have to say. You have not yet moved, but your speech has begun. Everything you say or do from that point onward may help or hurt.

As an experienced speaker, you will begin to establish audience contact immediately, following a procedure something like the following:

1. *Rise and move to the speaker's stand with dignity and confidence.* The rate at which you walk is important and should be in keeping with the mood in which you plan to begin your speech. Move too slowly, and people may think you are frightened. On the other hand, a mad dash up the three or four steps to the platform may leave you breathless. Be brisk but businesslike.

2. *Turn and face the audience, establishing contact with your feet and with your eyes.* Show by your stance that you are in command of the situation and expect attention. Meet their eyes directly and confidently.

3. *Keep the hands in the normal position unless you want them to be noticed at this point.* Sometimes the use of a chart or blackboard drawing may require some preliminary actions before you begin to speak. However, an audience will not watch you silently drawing for more than a few seconds before their attention will wander to other things. You may begin to move in some way, then, but your words will have to follow almost immediately.

4. *Establish contact with your mind, spending a second in sizing up your audience.* Think the opening words you planned to say before you pronounce them. Let the sense of anticipation rise in your listeners before you begin. Your sense of time will probably be distorted because you are under tension. What seems like a second to your audience may seem almost an hour to you. Never let your hearers feel that you had to start talking because you were too nervous to be quiet. Be sure you have their attention and that they are ready to listen; then begin.

5. *Establish contact with your voice with the very first words of your speech.* Every sound should be heard. Try to radiate the same confidence which you have just sought to exhibit in your appearance and actions. Then maintain this same sense of direct and immediate contact throughout the entire speech.

Break the contact. The speech should end in the same direct and dignified manner in which it began. The expert speaker does not just run down like an old phonograph. He comes to his prepared stopping place and brings the speech to an end. The following procedures may help you break contact with the audience at the conclusion of your speeches:

1. *Break contact with your voice.* The last words of the speech should be as carefully planned as the first words. Make sure your listeners can hear them; don't let your voice trail off in a faint mumble of sound. Say what you have to say, resist the temptation to add something more which may occur to you at the moment, and then be silent.

2. *Hold your last gesture for an instant longer than you normally would.* "Freeze" in position as you finish speaking. If you have ended with your hands in the normal position, keep them still for one instant more.

3. *Break contact with your eyes.* For these last seconds you have been particularly careful to look directly into the eyes of the people before you. Hold their gaze for a second or two after your last word has been pronounced. Then turn away from them to resume your seat.

4. *Break contact with your feet.* Your posture will have been straight and erect throughout the conclusion of the speech. You will work to maintain that same vital, alert appearance for that last second or two after you have said the last word. Then, as you drop your eyes, you will turn and begin to move toward your seat in the same dignified way in which you approached the speaker's stand at the beginning. Incidentally, you should begin to walk with the foot on the side toward which you are moving. Begin with the right foot if going to the right, with the left foot if going to the left. Crossing one foot over the other looks very awkward.

5. *Break contact with your mind.* If you expect your audience to be thinking of what you have said, you should concentrate on those last ideas also. Let your own attention wander for just an instant at the end, and the audience will begin to question whether you really meant what you said. Center your mind upon

your message and your listeners until you are back in your seat and the attention of the audience has been diverted to other things.

Real speaking is speaking to an audience. A speech doesn't really exist on paper, in your study, or in front of a mirror as you practice. Speaking is an event which happens between speaker and listener at a given time and place and upon a specific occasion. That event requires more than the mere physical presence of a person standing and talking while others are seated within range of his voice. Speaking assumes an interchange among the minds thus represented, a contact between speaker and listeners. The primary responsibility for establishing and maintaining this contact rests with you as the speaker. Both the content and the delivery of your speech should help you in fulfilling that responsibility.

PROJECTS AND ASSIGNMENTS

Supplementary Reading in the Speech Texts

Aristotle, *The Rhetoric,* Book II: Chapters 12-18.

Brigance, *Speech: Its Techniques and Disciplines in a Free Society,* Ch. 6: The People to Whom You Talk.

Bryant and Wallace, *Fundamentals of Public Speaking,* Ch. 18: The Audience: Motives and Basic Lines of Thought; Ch. 19: The Audience: Partisans, Neutrals, Opponents.

Sarett, *Basic Principles of Speech,* Ch. 13: Adapting Ideas: Principles and Methods.

Supplementary Reading in the Preaching Texts

Farmer, *The Servant of the Word,* Ch. 2: The I-Thou Relationship; Ch. 3: Preaching as Personal Encounter.

Garrison, *The Preacher and His Audience,* Ch. 2: Motivation of Preacher and Listener; Ch. 4: Attention of the Listener.

Thompson, *A Listener's Guide to Preaching,* Ch. 5: Listening to the Sermon.

Writing Assignment

Discuss one of the following topics:
1. What the Speaker Should Know About His Audience
2. Speaking the Language of Your Listeners
3. Varieties of Church Congregations
4. Reaching the Audience Through the Delivery of the Speech
5. Audience Analysis: Before, During, and After Speaking
6. The Influence of Audience Adaptation on Sermon Content

Speaking Assignment

Prepare and deliver a speech of 5 to 6 minutes in length on a subject of your own choosing. This speech should be of the same general nature (but not necessarily the same subject area) as your previous prepared speech. This time, be certain to include the proper transitional elements at every point where they are needed. Write the word "transition" on your outline at these points. Then write a one-sentence transition which you might use at each of those points. You will not be required to repeat that identical transition when you deliver the speech, but you should be certain to include *some* transition whenever one is needed. Follow the model below, adapting it to fit the number of mainheads and subheads which you have in your speech:

Title: _____

I. Introduction
   Method to be used: _____
   Transition: (Reference to time, occasion, place, etc.)
II. Central Idea: _____
   Transition: _____ (Repeat central idea) _____
III. Body
   Mainhead A _____
    Material to be used: _____
   Transition: _____ (Repeat central idea and Mainhead A) _____
   Mainhead B _____
   Transition: _____ (Repeat Mainhead B) _____
    1. _____
     Material to be used: _____
   Transition: _____ (Repeat 1 and B) _____

2. _____
      Material to be used: _____
   Transition: _____ (Repeat 1, 2, and B) _____
   3. _____
      Material to be used: _____
   Transition: _____ (Repeat 1, 2, 3, central idea, A and B) ____
   Mainhead C _____
      Material to be used: _____
   Transition: _____ (Repeat central idea and three mainheads) ____
IV. Conclusion
   Method to be used: (The summary is not to be used) ____

Since this speech calls for a transition between the last mainhead and the conclusion, a summary conclusion is *not* to be used. Any other method will be accepted.

You should be aware that the model outline used in this assignment is rather unusual in that it calls for the transitions to be written. Since a transition is an internal summary and the points included in any summary are obvious on an outline, speakers almost never bother to write out their transitions unless they are doing a full manuscript. The requirement was included in this assignment in order to impress upon you the necessity of including the transition in the speech. Future assignments need not have the transitions written on the outlines. Do not, however, omit them from the speech.

Deliver this speech, including all of the transitions, so that the parts will stand out clearly for the audience.

Listening Assignment

1. In class, listen carefully to all the other speakers. List the following points for each:
   a. The technique used in the speech introduction.
   b. The statement of the central idea.
   c. The statement of each mainhead and subhead used.
   d. The technique used in the speech conclusion.
   e. A note as to any point in the speech where a transition was needed but not used.

2. Outside of class, listen to some other speaker in a formal speech situation. Write a brief report of his speech which includes the following points:

 a. The facts about speaker, audience, time, occasion, etc.

 b. The assumptions which the speaker made about his audience— their age, sex, intelligence, interests, etc. Do you think his audience analysis was accurate? Why?

 c. An evaluation of the speaker's audience contact.

6

Getting Your Ideas Across

The act of speech involves one basic objective. The speaker has an idea in mind. His objective is to create that identical idea in the mind of his listener. The mechanical process involved is complex, but it may be described briefly. The speaker has a concept in mind—"Henry is a devout Christian." He changes this idea, which probably already exists in English words, into a series of nerve impulses to the muscles of his abdomen, chest, throat, and lower face. Air comes rushing out of his lungs, carrying the vibrations of the sounds, "Henry is a devout Christian." These vibrations travel through the air and strike the eardrums of another person, setting up nerve impulses that reach his brain. In less time than the process takes to describe, the listener has received the message, "Henry is a devout Christian."

If the speaker's articulation is careful and his listener's hearing is unimpaired, the message will be received. But has the speaker really succeeded in creating the identical thought in the mind of his listener? Consider some of the difficulties. First, both must be in agreement as to the "Henry" being discussed. Next, both must understand the same meaning for "devout"—which may range all the way from frequent church attendance to virtual sainthood. Finally, both must agree on precisely what they mean by "Christian."

Even if their understanding of these critical terms happens to be identical (which it never is), the speaker has still conveyed only an intellectual concept to his listener. The communication is still on the level of a mathematical statement: two and two make four. Most human communication is far richer in meaning than this. The term "Henry" carries with it all of one's feelings about the person, all of the history of their relationship. The speaker's whole reaction to him is embodied in the name. In the same way, the term "Christian" carries with it a whole set of emotional reactions, and the word "devout" adds still others. Our language is connotative as well as denotative. Our attempts to create in the minds of our hearers ideas identical to ours must somehow involve all of these emotions and experiences that cluster around every term that we use. Then the very relationship which these terms acquire when we place them together in a sentence adds additional feelings and emotions.

The listener is not simply a recorder who transcribes the messages that he receives. He is also a living person, with emotions and past experiences stored up around the various terms of the language. He has feelings about "Henry" and "devout" and "Christian" which may be very different from those of the speaker. Since each listener is a unique individual, each listener will have different feelings about every one of these terms. The communication of a simple proposition to an audience of any size thus becomes a matter of immense difficulty.

How, then, can we get the members of our audience to see matters as we see them when we combine our simple propositions into speeches? Everything that we say is conditioned by who we are, our family background, the things we have read and seen and heard, and all of the experiences that we have had. In the same way, everything that each member of the audience hears is conditioned by the sum total of his past experiences. If we would get another person to see things as we see them and to believe what we believe, we must make that person a twin brother to ourselves, one who has experienced everything that we have experienced and who has reacted in an identical way.

In spite of such considerations, we do succeed, within limits, in communicating our thoughts and feelings. We recognize that our hearers will never get the exact message that we seek to transmit to them, with all of the emotions we associate with the ideas we seek to convey. We do, however, communicate enough of our ideas and their related feelings to achieve a general correspondence of thought between us and our listeners. Our success is due to three basic procedures; our improvement in communication will be due to our increased efficiency in handling these processes.

First, the speaker maintains audience contact so that he is aware of communication difficulties as they arise. The feedback, or information coming back to the speaker, makes him aware of the existence and, to some extent, the source of these problems and enables him to compensate for them. For instance, suppose the wails of a baby interfere with the words of a preacher. His ears make him aware of the noise, and his eyes reveal that some in the congregation can no longer hear him. Immediately, he increases the volume of his voice, reduces his rate of speaking, and becomes more physically active to hold the wandering attention of his hearers. In a similar manner the speaker may compensate for mental as well as physical blocks in the communication process. Thus if you would improve your ability to communicate, improve your audience contact.

Second, the speaker expresses his ideas in words and phrases which his listeners will understand. In place of "Henry is a devout Christian," he might say, "Henry Jones is a genuine saint," or he "has a Christlike character." In theory, the speaker knows his audience and chooses language to express his thoughts which will most nearly evoke identical thoughts in their minds. The subject of speech style, the clothing of thought in language, will be considered in a later chapter. For the present, remember the principle that the speaker who communicates is one who expresses his ideas in words which will be understood as nearly as possible as he understands them.

The third procedure is for the speaker to share some of his experience as well as his ideas. The meaning which he associates with the words he chooses has been built up in his own mind out of all his accumulated perceptions in the past. Let him share some of that past experience with his audience so that they may, to a degree, share his thought. He cannot make them relive a portion of his past life, but he can put that experience into words and convey it, along with his basic idea, to his audience. He cannot relate all of the events of the past, but he can select those which have a bearing on the idea he is trying to communicate. By sharing experiences the speaker comes closer to his goal of shared meaning. These condensed experiences, expressed in words for the purpose of putting over or making vivid an idea, are called the *speech materials.*

Speech materials have probative as well as communicative value. They constitute evidence upon which a conclusion is based. Your listener may know perfectly well what you mean when you speak to him of Henry's devotion, but he doesn't agree with you. He feels that Henry is a hypocrite and that your assessment of his character is in error. Before you convince him, you will need to share with him the evidence upon which your conclusion is based. This evidence will be condensed experiences, expressed in words for the purpose of offering logical proof of the proposition you are advocating. Thus in the last analysis your argument will rest on these same speech materials.

IDENTIFYING THE SPEECH MATERIALS

The classification of speech materials is not easy. The various categories tend to overlap. In addition, some of these items may also be classified as stylistic devices, functions of language, rather than vehicles of experience. Nevertheless, the following listing is representative and should be useful:

1. *Restatement.* The speaker makes his idea vivid by repeating it, sometimes in the same words, but often in different words. For example:

Idea: Religion is the hope of mankind.
Restatement: As we look at man with all of his fears and frustrations, we realize that only through religion can he gain any faith in the future.

2. *Explanation.* The speaker uses additional words to give details. He amplifies the idea, gives more information about the concepts and relationships involved. For example:

Idea: Love can overlook human failures.
Explanation: All of us make mistakes from time to time; none of us is perfect. Every human being will have flaws in his character, and these flaws will cause errors in judgment and mistakes in behavior. But the person who is loving is able to overlook these human mistakes and maintain a warm, affectionate relationship in spite of them.

3. *Definition.* The speaker may be using some term in the statement of his idea which will be unfamiliar to his audience. He pauses to clear up the meaning of this term as he is using it. The definition may be a formal one quoted from a dictionary or an informal expression of the particular sense in which the speaker intends to use the word. For example:

Idea: Religion is an asset to the human race.
Definition: By "religion" I do not refer to little creeds and dogmas but to all of that great body of truth that man has built up in his never-ending search for God.

The preceding three materials—restatement, explanation, and definition—are sometimes grouped and called the "general processes." They are very closely related to some aspects of style.

4. *Illustration*. The speaker gives a case, an incident, an event, to throw light upon the idea he wants to convey. An effective speaker will relate the experience in as graphic a manner as possible, giving as many details as he can. An illustration is an example which serves to demonstrate the point. The case may be actual or hypothetical, dramatic or matter-of-fact, humorous or serious. Illustrations are complete enough to illuminate the principle being discussed, in contrast to *instances* which are briefer references to similar cases or events.

Idea: The Christian has hope, even in the face of death.

Illustration: The account of an accident in which a young husband and father lost his life. The wife found comfort and hope in her faith whereas the parents became angry and bitter. The story should be as complete as possible without betraying any confidences, including the details of what took place and what happened afterward. The speaker must supply enough facts to demonstrate the relationship between the story and the idea being illustrated and enough facts to hold the attention of the audience. He should not, however, allow the illustration to become so detailed that the story detracts attention from the basic idea. The details included should be pertinent details.

If the speaker does not have knowledge of a case from his own personal experience, he may substitute one from some other source. If he is unable to find a positive illustration, he may use a negative one—perhaps the case of an individual who was unable to cope with some tragic experience in life because he lacked a religious faith. If the speaker cannot give an actual case—positive or negative—to illustrate the point, he may invent a hypothetical illustration to serve instead. In doing so, he could not ethically present the hypothetical case as literal fact. He might begin by saying, "Let us suppose that a certain individual goes to his doctor for an ordinary physical checkup only to be told that he has contracted a disease which gives him only a few weeks to live. Such an individual might . . ." At the same

time, the hypothetical illustration must be true to life or it will
have no illustrative force.

These actual experiences are probably the most important of
all of the speech materials. They enable the audience to share in
events and feelings related to the point the speaker wants to
convey. If they are dramatic and well told, they arouse curiosity
and increase interest. If they also include the element of humor,
they elicit an overt response from the hearers (their laughter)
and leave the audience more open to suggestion and to persuasion. The illustration is so important that you are urged to
adopt the following rule for all of your speaking: *Any point
worth talking about is worth a detailed illustration.*

5. *Instance.* The speaker makes reference to a case or event
which throws light on the idea he wants to convey. The instance
is like an illustration in all respects except in length. The speaker's assumption is that the members of the audience already know
the case to which he refers. To tell the story in detail would thus
be a waste of time. He only mentions the case briefly in order
to call it to the attention of his hearers and to get them to see
its relationship to the idea which he is trying to convey.

As a general rule, the illustration is used to give interest and
impact to the idea being presented. The audience is made to see
it in operation as it actually happened or might have happened.
The instance is used to deepen or reinforce the initial impression.
One case has little value as proof, for it might be one case in a
million—the exception that proves the rule. Additional instances
of the same principle make it seem much more likely to the
skeptical members of the audience.

6. *Comparison and contrast.* The speaker points out the likenesses (comparison) or differences (contrast) between two
things, persons, or events in order to establish or make vivid the
point he is trying to convey. The illustration given above, for
example, would become a contrast if the speaker placed his

emphasis on the difference between the reactions of the wife and the parents to the tragedy. Thus the comparison or contrast may be regarded as a double illustration or instance, with two people or events recounted in order to emphasize likeness or difference. The comparison frequently serves as the basis for an argument: Our church is like a certain other congregation. They increased attendance by using newspaper advertising; therefore, we should use newspaper advertising also. Such an argument may be logically strong if significant likenesses can be established.

7. *Analogy.* The speaker finds some artificial point of likeness between things that are actually quite different. Thus, the analogy is a comparison of unlike things, persons, or events. The analogy of the builders found in Matthew 7:24-27 is one example. The man who hears and obeys the message is like a man building a house upon a rock foundation. The analogy or parable was common in the teaching of Jesus, and it can be used just as effectively today.

The analogy is also closely related to certain aspects of style. You have probably already recognized that it is nothing more than an extended simile. It is unlike the comparison in that it has very little probative value. The things it compares are, by definition, unlike things. The likeness exists in the mind of the speaker and not in the things or events themselves. Thus, what is true about one thing proves absolutely nothing about the other. The analogy is used to clarify, not to prove.

8. *Quotation.* The speaker uses the words of another to make his idea more vivid or to appropriate the authority of the other person in support of the idea. The language in which an idea is phrased may make it more appealing to the members of the audience. Don't hesitate to use the language of another (always giving proper credit, of course) to express your thoughts more graphically. Some speakers will use a brief quotation as a refrain

which they repeat again and again throughout the speech. Ministers often use this technique in preaching, taking some brief phrase of scripture as a text and repeating it throughout the sermon.

The quotation has such value as proof of a speaker's contentions that it is the chief material used by lawyers in court. Almost their entire argument may be based on the testimony of witnesses and the quotations from previous decisions in similar cases. The speaker who uses the quotation presents similar "testimony" to the members of his audience. Naturally, he tries to be sure that: (a) the man quoted is free from bias or special interest; (b) the man quoted is of good character; (c) the man quoted is in a position to know the facts; (d) the quotation is not inconsistent with his other statements; (e) the quotation is not inconsistent with the statements of other authorities; (f) the quotation is a serious statement, made with full knowledge of the implications of what was said. A quotation meeting all of these requirements would have great logical force in proving the point being supported. The reluctant admission of an opponent of any viewpoint also has unusual value in supporting that viewpoint.

9. *Statistics.* The speaker presents factual information which is numerical in nature to support his point. The relation between cigarette smoking and the incidence of lung cancer, for instance, must ultimately rest on this type of evidence. Statistics are similar to the quotation in that their logical value as proof is no greater than the authority supplying them. In addition, statistical material must receive especially careful evaluation in terms of audience interest. Numbers are abstract and nonhuman. People are more interesting than things, and things are more interesting than abstractions. Thus statistics should not be overused. Ordinarily, you will want to cite round numbers so that the audience can grasp them easily. You may also want to combine statistics with an illustration or a comparison in order to maintain interest. For instance, you could compare the 50,000 people

who die in traffic accidents in this country each year with the total destruction of some specific city of that size by an atomic bomb. Dry as statistics may often be, they are frequently vital for both exposition and argumentation.

10. *The audio-visual aid.* The speaker supplies the audience with visual or auditory experiences which serve directly to make his idea vivid for his listeners. He may show them an actual object or a picture or diagram. Even abstract concepts may be pictured on a chart. The speaker may manipulate the object or model as he explains it so that the talk becomes a demonstration of the point in question. The audio-visual aid may appeal to the ear instead of the eye, as in the case of a speaker who plays snatches of music on a phonograph to illustrate his speech. Or the material may be literally audio-visual, as when the speaker uses an extract from a sound motion picture.

The audio-visual aid, strictly speaking, is separate from the speaker's own voice, physical presence, or gestures as he delivers the speech. A gesture to indicate the size of an object being discussed would not be a visual aid in this sense. The actual object, held up for inspection, would be a visual aid. Neither should the audio-visual aid be confused with the stage setting in which a speaker talks. The picture of a candidate, for instance, prominently displayed on the platform, would not be a visual aid unless the speaker were to use it to argue that the firm jaw denoted determination. The cross on a church altar is not a visual aid, even though the sermon gives its chief attention to the subject of the cross. The preacher could, however, utilize the same cross as a visual aid by pointing to it and reminding his congregation of the manner in which the arms seem to reach out to encircle all mankind.

Although no speaker should give the impression of being encumbered by gadgets or "choked" by charts, the imagination of the speaker is about the only limit to the number of audio-visual aids that are possible in a given speech. The rules for the use and misuse of such objects are almost as varied as the items possible for use. However, the following principles may prove helpful to you:

1. *The visual aid should be an aid;* it should not take over the entire speech. Beware of the phonograph and the motion-picture projector which can easily outweigh the speaker. If you draw on a blackboard, draw rapidly and roughly. Don't worry about the quality of your art; clarify the point and move on with the speech.

2. *Do nothing to endanger an audience, or even to make them fearful of possible danger.* Never use an actual firearm; a picture or model will suffice. Be careful of fire and of pets which may become excited. Some members of the audience may be subject to heart attacks if frightened by a sudden action or loud noise. If your visual aid constitutes a threat, even an imaginary one, to the audience, they will be unable to concentrate on the significance of the object being used.

3. *Don't let the audio-visual aid break audience contact.* Be sure that the thing you are showing can be easily seen or heard by all members of the audience. If a picture is too small, project it on a screen. If an object is too complex, show the audience a diagram which simplifies the process. Continue to speak all the time you are manipulating the object or drawing on the blackboard. Remember that your primary focus of attention is on the audience, not on the visual aid. Practice until you can keep your eyes on the audience most of the time. If the process you are demonstrating takes a period of time, don't make your audience wait. Prepare a number of visual aids showing the various stages of the process so that you can move rapidly from one to the next.

4. *The audio-visual aid must not conflict with the mood of the entire speech.* It must be suitable to the speaker, the subject matter, the audience, and the occasion. A preacher talking to a primary class in his Sunday school might find a visual aid very

helpful. The same object could alienate or insult an audience of adults at the morning worship service.

5. *Don't arouse more curiosity than you can satisfy.* A visual aid that does so becomes a distraction rather than an aid. Sometimes a model or diagram may be more suitable for your speech than the actual object. The object may have additional aspects which will distract the audience from the one thing being discussed. Beware of using animals or children in a demonstration; they often cause the speaker to lose control of the entire situation. If another adult is going to help you with a demonstration, be sure that he is well rehearsed to do his part and no more! If your speech involves an object which is edible (cake, cookies, candy, and the like), bring enough for a sample for each one of your listeners. Don't leave them curious about the quality of the end product after the process has been explained.

These ten types of material serve to put over or make vivid the speaker's ideas. The discussion is not complete, however, until we specify what we mean by "putting over" an idea. Unless you as a speaker understand precisely what you must do to transmit your ideas in the fullness of their denotative and connotative meanings to the audience, you will be handicapped in the selection of the materials that you will need.

USING THE SPEECH MATERIALS

The process of putting over a single idea to the audience involves the following distinct steps, in this order:

1. *The clarification of the idea.* The audience must understand exactly what the point is that you are trying to make, whether they agree with it or not.

2. *The verification of the idea.* The audience must sense that what you're saying is true, or that it happened at least once in history, at some specific time and place. They may doubt that

your principle is a common occurrence, but they cannot doubt that it happened at least once.

3. *The amplification of the idea.* The audience must be brought to agree that your principle frequently holds true. It is the rule, not the exception.

4. *The application of the idea.* The audience must see the relevance of your idea. They must understand what it has to do with them, and they should see what they ought to do about it. The application answers the question, "So what?"

As the speaker discusses his point, he will select the specific kinds of material that he needs to accomplish each one of these four steps. He might proceed somewhat as follows:

Statement of the idea being presented
  (Clarification)
    Restatement—to be certain all have heard
    Explanation—if the idea is complicated
    Definition—if unfamiliar terms are used
  (Verification)
    Illustration
    Instance
    Comparison or contrast
    Analogy
    Visual aid
  (Amplification)
    Additional instances
    Quotation
    Statistics
    Visual aid
  (Application)
    Explanation of the relationship to the audience
    Illustration
    Analogy
    Visual aid

This scheme merely indicates the common use of each of the speech materials. In actual practice, almost any type of material could be used in carrying out any of the four steps in the discussion of an idea.

In your speeches, you will not need to follow a scheme as complete as this one for every point. Some ideas need very little in the way of verification or amplification. If you are speaking to inform the audience, the clarification of each point and its application to the individuals before you may be all that is necessary. In addition, whatever your general purpose, you would use only the materials that are really necessary to clarify, verify, amplify, and apply your point. The use of additional, unnecessary material would waste time and might make the audience feel that you are talking down to them. Finally, your discussion will always be limited by the material actually available for the development of each point. Sometimes even a great deal of reading and research will fail to provide you with the exact quotation or illustration that you feel you would like to have for one point or another. In such a case, you must make do with whatever material seems to be available.

You should now have clearly in mind the two alternatives which we discussed earlier for the communication of ideas to listeners. First, an idea may be communicated by means of analysis—dividing it into parts so that the understanding of all of the parts will result in the understanding of the whole. Second, an idea may be communicated by means of shared experience— by recounting the various definitions and illustrations, analogies and visual aids, and all of the other speech materials that we have listed. The first alternative may be regarded as preparatory. Ideas which are too large and complex must be analyzed into their simple parts for purposes of communication. The actual transfer of thought from the mind of the speaker to the mind of the listener must be based on the second alternative, that of shared experience. Ultimately, no matter how much a central idea might be divided into mainheads, mainheads into subheads, and subheads into sub-subheads, the speaker must turn to the speech materials in order to communicate his ideas. Let him turn experience into words and transmit those words to the ears and minds of his listeners. They may then come to share the experience, and in that sharing they may create in their minds an idea which is very close to the one the speaker is trying to convey.

Each speaker, therefore, must understand the difference between a subdivision of his speech and the various materials that he may use to communicate that subdivision. At this point you probably feel that the difference is obvious. Who would ever confuse a humorous illustration with a subhead? But matters are not always that simple. You may often find yourself puzzled as you try to decide whether one portion of your speech consists of a series of instances or a series of subdivisions. Part of the success of your speech may depend upon the decision that you make. If you really have a series of instances, no further development may be necessary; perhaps you can proceed directly to the next point. On the other hand, a series of subheads would require some sort of speech material to convey them to the audience. You should also remember that transitions would be necessary between subdivisions, whereas no such internal summaries would be required between instances. The ability to distinguish between points and materials is thus very basic and very vital. It is a skill which you will develop as you gain experience and continue to devote yourself to the task of handling and communicating ideas.

In order to speed your learning, you must make a clear-cut decision each time the problem is before you: Is this specific item a piece of speech material or a sub-point? If it is material, how should it be classified? If it is a point, what other points are coordinate with it? (Note that nothing can be divided into one division. If you have actually divided something, you must have at least two pieces. For this reason, an outline should never have an "A" without a "B" or a "1" without a "2.") Our attempts to force you to confront such decisions as these give rise to a peculiarity of this book which you may have already noticed. All of the outline points given, in the assignments or elsewhere, are designated by the usual signs of A, B, C, 1, 2, 3, etc. The materials given underneath these points are never designated by such signs. Now that you have learned to identify the various types of material, you can designate each of them by name, inserting the label of the type of material which you plan to use at the proper point on the outline. Such a procedure means that every item on every outline will confront you with the same decision: Is this a point, or is it a piece of material? If it is a point, it will be identified by the appropriate outline designation. It will have coordinate points, and it will require transitions when the speech is delivered. It should have some sort of speech material beneath it. If it is a piece of material, it will be identified on the outline by the appropriate label. It will not require coordinate items, and full transitions will not be necessary when you deliver the speech.

Let each of your outlines represent your best efforts at trying to distinguish between points and materials. Note these examples:

Wrong

III. Body
    A. Statement of first mainhead
        1. Illustration of this mainhead
    B. Statement of second mainhead
        1. Subdivision
            a. Explanation
            b. Visual aid—blackboard drawing
        2. Subdivision
            a. Definition
            b. Illustration of this subdivision

Right

III. Body
    A. Statement of first mainhead
        Illustration of this mainhead (Include a few words indicating what this illustration is about.)

B. Statement of second mainhead
  1. Subdivision
      Explanation
      Visual aid—blackboard drawing
  2. Subdivision
      Definition (Indicate the word being defined.)
      Illustration of this subdivision (include a few words indicating what this illustration is about.)

Note that the correct outline portion clearly differentiates between the points (which take the ordinary outline designations) and the materials (indicated by the labels). Also notice the manner in which we have solved the little logical problem previously mentioned, in outlining mainhead A. The "wrong" outline uses the figure "1" under this mainhead, thus raising the question of the whereabouts of part "2" of that division. The truth of the matter is that part "2" does not exist because part "1" is not a true division at all. The "right" outline avoids the entire problem by refusing to use the "1" when no division is intended.

In summary, then, you should use a standard form for your outlines. The usual method is as follows:

I.
II.
  A.
  B.
    1.
    2.
      a.
      b.
        (1)
        (2)
          (a)
          (b)

Identify each type of material that you plan to use. Place the label for that type in the appropriate place on your outline. Be careful to differentiate between divisions and these materials by reserving the outline signs for the points and by reserving the labels for the materials. Keep in mind, as you prepare each speech, the fact that the full communication of each idea requires the clarification, verification, amplification, and application of that point. The materials are the shared experiences that you use to accomplish this communication. In all things, work to be clear, to be logical, and to be relevant.

PROJECTS AND ASSIGNMENTS

Supplementary Reading in the Speech Texts

Bryant and Wallace, *Fundamentals of Public Speaking,* Ch. 7: Amplification in Informative Speaking; Ch. 8: Visual Aids to Amplification.
Weaver, *Speaking in Public,* Ch. 8: Developing the Speech; Ch. 18: Visual Aids.
White, *Practical Public Speaking,* Ch. 6: Developing the Body of the Speech: Understanding Principles.

Supplementary Reading in the Preaching Texts

Bryan, *The Art of Illustrating Sermons,* Ch. 3: Varieties of Illustrations and Their Use; Ch. 7: Building Illustrations into Sermons.
Jeffs, *The Art of Sermon Illustration,* Ch. 2: General Principles of Illustration.
Whitesell and Perry, *Variety in Your Preaching,* Ch. 6: Vary the Supporting Material in Your Sermons; Ch. 7: Vary the Illustrations in Your Sermons; Ch. 11: Vary the Methods of Presenting Your Sermons.

Writing Assignment

Discuss one of the following topics:
1. The Illustration in Speech and Sermon
2. Lying with Statistics
3. The Use and Misuse of Visual Aids

4. Making Your Ideas Apply to Your Audience
5. What Constitutes "an Authority"?
6. Prophets, Preachers, and Visual Aids

Speaking Assignment

Prepare and deliver a speech of 5 to 6 minutes in length on a subject of your own choosing. This speech should be of the same general nature as your previous speeches but should meet the following additional requirements:

1. The general purpose of this speech must be *to inform*.

2. You must use one or more audio-visual aids somewhere in this speech.

3. Make your outline complete by listing each type of material by name at the point in the outline where it belongs. (Note: Do not use outline designations for these materials. They are not subdivisions but simply the materials used to convey the points or ideas to the audience.)

4. Follow the sample outline which follows. Naturally, you do not need to use all of the materials indicated under each division. Your time is limited, and the available materials are probably limited also. The sample outline simply includes a representative list of materials similar to what you *might* have. However, you *must* have an audio-visual aid somewhere in the introduction, conclusion, or body of the speech. (You may use it throughout the speech, if you wish.) Also notice the blanks on the sample outline which indicate that your outline should have more than just the label of the material you intend to use. Include also a few words indicating *what* word you are going to define, *what* illustration you plan to tell, or *what* instance you expect to use.

Title: _____
I. Introduction
   Method to be used: _____

II. Central Idea: _____

III. Body
   Mainhead A _____
      Explanation _____
      Definition _____

Illustration _____

Visual aid _____

Instance _____

Statistics _____

Mainhead B _____

1. _____

    Definition _____

    Restatement

    Illustration _____

    Visual aid _____

    Comparison _____

2. _____

    Explanation _____

    Illustration _____

    Analogy _____

    Visual aid _____

    Quotation "_____"

IV. Conclusion

    Method to be used: _____

Since this speech is planned *to inform,* careful transitions will be needed; but they should not be written on the outline.

Rehearse this speech carefully, particularly your handling of the audio-visual aids. Deliver it so that your ideas will be absolutely clear to the audience.

Listening Assignment

1. In class, make a complete outline of the messages delivered by the other speakers. List all of the ideas of the speeches, including central ideas, main divisions, and subdivisions. Identify each type of speech material used by the other speakers, placing the label identifying the type on your outlines at the point where each piece of material was used. Try to make your outline of each speech approximate the original outline which the speaker must have prepared beforehand.

2. Outside of class, listen to some speaker in a formal speech situation. Note the facts about speaker, audience, time, etc. Organize your notes on this speech in the following manner:

a. A point made by the speaker
b. Materials used to clarify this point
c. Materials used to verify this point
d. Materials used to amplify this point
e. Materials used to apply this point.

List the materials in this manner for each point that the speaker makes. Note particularly the points where the speaker uses no materials at all to perform one of the four functions. Try to decide the reason for the omission. Did the speaker err, or was the function unnecessary in this particular case? Why?

7

Your Speech Delivery

Even the most careful speech planning is wasted unless the ideas are conveyed to the eyes and ears of the audience. The most dramatic illustration will have no effect if the people cannot hear the speaker. The most powerful argument will lose its influence if the speaker's posture conveys the idea that the whole matter is of little importance anyway. The average person will expend little effort in trying to understand someone else. If you speak as though you have mush in your mouth, most of your listeners will be quite content to concentrate on their own concerns and let you chew your oatmeal in peace.

Every speech delivered in the usual speech situation will have two avenues of approach to each normal member of the audience. One transmission line will run through the ear, for speech communicates meaning through sounds. A second avenue will ordinarily be open, that of the eye; and let a speaker never forget that "actions speak louder than words." Both lines of communication should agree in what they convey. The speech that the audience sees should agree with the speech that they hear, and both of these should bear a reasonable similarity to the speech that the speaker intended.

The study of voice and diction is often a complete college course, and professional actors continue to give attention to movement and gesture. A detailed analysis of these areas would be out of place here. Nevertheless, a few words of instruction might help to make you conscious of your weaknesses and to encourage you to work to improve the way you sound and the way you look. Keep in mind the various aspects of your speech which your hearers will be certain to notice:

Your lips speak. Let the sounds be formed so perfectly that no one can mistake them. Of course, the tongue and teeth must function properly as well as the lips. Listen to the way you pronounce "s" in phrases like "slim, slick, slender saplings." Is it a tiny, distinct, sharp hiss? Can the ears of the listener distinguish it from "sh" or "th"? And what about the "r" sound in an expression like "round, red rock"? You should feel it in the front of your mouth, not caught like a bone in the back of your throat. Remember that these sounds should also maintain their individual, distinct quality when they appear in the middle of a word or at the end of a phrase.

What about that final "ng" sound? Do you say "going," "coming," "hunting," "fishing," or is it "goin," "comin," "huntin," fishin"? Do your hearers become confused about such words as "weather" and "whether," or "then" and "thin"? Do you omit sounds entirely in words like "government," "February," "picture," "library," and "arctic"? (Not "goverment," "Febawary," "piture"—which will be confused with "pitcher"—"liberry," and "artic.") Use the whole mechanism of articulation to produce each sound clearly and distinctly, so that it will not be confused with any other sound in the language.

Make a recording of your speech, and listen to yourself carefully. Raise the following questions:

Do I distort sounds? Do such consonants as "r" and "s" seem normal?

Do I omit sounds? Check the final sound in words which end your phrases and sentences. Are they really there? Notice words like "didn't" and "couldn't." Do these become "di–n't" or "cou–n't"? (Technically, you may be substituting a glottal stop for the "d.")

Do I add sounds? Do I add a little grunt at the ends of words, saying "men-uh" and "women-uh"? Do I say "ath-a-lete" instead of "athlete"?

Do I substitute one sound for another, saying "you howwible wabbit" or "thister Thuzy thells thea shells"?

Do I unvoice final sounds so that the final "d" becomes a "t" or the final "z" becomes an "s"? Remember that words like "houses" and "horses" actually end in "z" sounds.

Do I exaggerate sounds, holding on to final "m," "n," and "ng" until I seem to intone these endings?

Do I shift vowels? Do words like "condition" and "contrition" sound like "condeetion" and "contreetion"? The word "fish" should not be "feesh." The "i" vowels should match the sound in "hit" and "bit."

Do I become sloppy in articulation, especially when speaking rapidly? Does that final "ng" become an "n"? Do I say "git" for "get" and "jist" for "just"? Identify your habitual errors; then concentrate on each one until you have eliminated it.

Your voice speaks as it conveys each shade of meaning expressed in your words. Think in terms of the four aspects of voice, and evaluate your ability to handle all four.

1. *The pitch of your voice.* Avoid the monotone, or people may find you monotonous. If your ideas are interesting, let the variations in the pitch of your voice convey that interest. Don't try to change the natural, basic pitch of the voice by forcing the tone higher or lower. Don't shriek. Greater volume need not be

accompanied by higher pitch. However, a voice that does not vary in pitch is unnatural.

Beware of the stereotyped pitch pattern which repeats itself in sentence after sentence. Concentrate on the meaning, and let the pitch of your voice express your ideas. One of the worst faults in the pulpit is what is called the "preacher's tone." Its most obvious characteristic is a habitual pitch pattern which makes statements sound like questions; that is, the preacher gives a rising inflection at the end of indicative sentences just as he would with interrogative sentences. For example, take the following familiar words: "The Lord is my shepherd; I shall not want. He maketh me . . ." First, read these words with a rising inflection on the words "shepherd" and "want." Imagine that they are punctuated by question marks: "The Lord is my shepherd? I shall not want?" What you are doing will be very close to the preacher's tone.

Now read those words again, letting your pitch drop. Make each expression a solid, definite statement of fact. Be certain; be positive. "The Lord *is* my shepherd! I shall *not* want." Imagine that you are asserting these facts in the face of someone who denies them. Move as far away from the uncertainty of the preacher's tone as you can get. Finally, read the words a third time, taking care to remove the feelings of belligerence or defensiveness but maintaining the same positive feeling you had on the second reading. Your pitch pattern should now be close to expressing the meaning of the words.

2. *The volume of your voice.* If you cannot be heard, you had better not speak at all. Audiences are frustrated and antagonized by the voice that hovers just below the threshold of audibility. In addition, you have no assurance that the members of your audience have normal hearing! Adopt a volume level that will allow you to be heard by those sitting on the back row. Then never let your volume drop below this level.

3. *The rate at which you speak.* Don't speak so slowly that attention can wander; don't speak so rapidly that you are difficult

to understand. Within these limits, let your voice vary in rate in the same manner that it varies in pitch. As a general rule, the thought structure of the speech—the central idea, mainheads, and subordinate points—should be presented slowly, forcefully, and distinctly. The speech materials should be presented more rapidly. An illustration should move so that the audience senses the flow of the narrative. Instances should take little time since they are brief in nature and probably already familiar to many in the audience. Simple explanations may also be rushed. Spend the time on those matters which are central in importance.

Most speakers will probably average between 120 and 150 words per minute. However, you cannot evaluate your speech rate by a simple word count; too many other factors are involved. The larger the hall and the larger the audience, the slower the rate should be. The speaker who uses a public-address system should also speak more slowly. The mood of the message is also important; a funeral certainly calls for a more deliberate pace than a youth rally. A complex argument should be presented more slowly than an after-dinner speech designed primarily to entertain.

One mark of the expert speaker is the ability to make effective use of the pause, that brief period of dead silence. Just as the amateur musician may be victimized by the rhythm pattern of his music so that variation becomes impossible, so the amateur speaker seems to fear a pause. And yet, such pauses may be some of the most effective instruments of speech delivery. They help to recapture the attention of people who have been hypnotized by the flow of language. They serve to emphasize important points. They heighten the dramatic effect of portions of the speech. Don't be afraid to pause, even when you know perfectly well what you are going to say next. Never show embarrassment at the pause which gives you a chance to think of what comes next, as when you face that common affliction of having your mind go blank. Above all, never vocalize a pause. Few things disturb an audience as quickly as the speaker who repeats "uh—

er—and–uh—un—ah" every few words. None of us is perfectly
fluent, and we all break the flow of language from time to time
as we search for the word that comes next. When such gaps
occur, however, let them be genuine; never fill them in with
meaningless sounds.

The basic objective of your speaking rate, as with the pitch
pattern of your voice, is to sound natural. Good conversational
speech is the ideal. Start from this basis; then exaggerate each
aspect of your voice to be congruent with the setting in which
you speak. As auditorium and audience become larger, pitch
variations will become wider, volume will be increased so that
all can hear, and the rate of speaking will become markedly
slower. Many speakers lose their sense of time when facing an
audience so that they must make a conscious, deliberate effort to
speak more slowly.

4. *The quality of your voice.* Try to produce a sound which is
reasonably pleasant for your hearers or, at least, one which does
not repel them. While the overall improvement of voice quality
is a matter requiring faithful, guided practice over the years, you
can reduce some of your worst faults by keeping a few simple
things in mind to guide your speaking. For one thing, have an
adequate breath supply and speak with a good flow of air. As
you take a breath, keep the expansion low—just above the belt-
line. Keep your throat relaxed and open as you speak; have the
feeling that you are about to yawn. Try to project your voice so
that its sound seems to be focused at your lips or beyond them,
out in front of your face. If your voice seems to be located back
in your throat, relax and let it come up and out. Don't be afraid
to open your lips; your vowels may come whining out of your
nose if your lips don't give them room to escape. Let the muscle
power for singing or speaking come from the abdominal muscles,
not from the muscles of your neck or upper chest.

Your social background speaks. You may not appreciate the
message it conveys. You are probably aware that the speech of

every individual will tell a great deal about the geographical area from which he comes and the cultural stratum of his family. We would not expect a resident of Mississippi to sound like a proper Bostonian. Neither would we want the pronunciation habits of any part of the country set up as an approved standard and forced on all of the rest of us. Nevertheless, in this day of a mobile population and in a country blanketed by radio and television, a speaker should not be identified too obviously with any small, peculiar speech area. A speech that is thoughtful and intelligent in content should be spoken in a manner that bears witness to a breadth of cultural and educational background.

Major regional differences need not concern you, so long as you follow the general pattern of the best speakers of your area. The average person need not tamper with his southern accent or eastern accent, even though he finds himself living in Seattle. However, the intrusive "r" in such expressions as "the *idear* of it" is not considered standard speech in any part of the country and represents a habit which should be overcome. Be sure that your regional differences can be defended as the best speech of a major region. You can, for example, make a good case for either pronunciation of the word "pecan"—to rhyme with "Ann," or to rhyme with "on." You may distinguish between "Mary," "merry," and "marry," or pronounce them all alike. However, don't change the vowel of "sit" so that it becomes "set," as many speakers do in the Southwest, or you will be criticized for your grammar as well as your pronunciation.

Examples of substandard regionalisms can be multiplied almost without end. "These," "those," and "them" should not be pronounced "dese," "dose," and "dem." The "t" is not pronounced in the word "often." Midwesterners will laugh at those who say "boid" in place of "bird." Let them be equally careful that they don't say "warship" in place of "worship." (It rhymes with "were.") May there be an extra star in the crown of the minister who pronounces "saith" to rhyme with "Beth." These are only a few of the common errors. Get a good, conservative dictionary and alter your pronunciation to conform to its standards.

Your appearance speaks. We expect men who stand on the public platform to have clean collars, pressed trousers, and polished shoes unless circumstances furnish an excuse. We expect a woman to be dressed simply and tastefully. Your audience will be annoyed and distracted by any failure on your part to meet these expectations. In most cases, your looks will influence your listeners before your words reach them.

No detail is too small to be overlooked. Hair should be neat and well-groomed. Women should avoid unusual or extreme hair styles. Men should shave closely to avoid that "five o'clock shadow." Avoid anything about the clothing or accessories that might distract an audience—a loud necktie, long and dangling earrings, bracelets that clatter with each movement of the arms. If you are being televised, obtain the services of a makeup expert. Don't make the mistake that Richard Nixon made in the first television debate of the 1960 presidential campaign when faulty makeup made him appear old and tired in contrast to the youthful Kennedy.

Aspects of appearance will communicate to the audience the type of person you are. If you slouch, drop one shoulder, and put your weight on one foot, the audience will know that you are a tired, lazy person—whether you are or not! On the other hand, if you stand like a statue, stiff and unmoving, they will know that you are timid and frightened. Let your appearance convey to the audience the impression of the warm, vivacious person you really are. Your whole muscle tone will play an important part. Be erect, alert, poised, ready for action. You are not a pile of putty dumped on the stage. You should be balanced like a boxer, with the boxer's ability to move any part of the body in any direction at any time.

Your movements speak. Any movements that you make before an audience, apart from the movements involved in the act of speaking itself, may be called "gestures." Such gestures, under this broad definition, will convey a message to the eyes of the audience at the same time that your voice is conveying a message to their ears. These two messages should agree, or people will be distracted and confused.

Some of these gestures will be aimless, purposeless, useless movements which you should work to eliminate entirely. One speaker may twist a ring; another will toy with a lock of hair; a third, holding a ball-point pen, may begin to click the point in and out as he speaks. Do any of these things, and your nervousness will be obvious to your audience. You may well be frightened as you speak, but you need not advertise that fact. Thank the kind friend who makes you aware of these unfortunate, habitual gestures; then put a stop to them.

Constructive movements or gestures in speaking may be classified into four groups. One contains the *indicative gestures,* those movements which draw the attention of the audience to physical things actually present in the room or to abstract concepts which are treated as physically present. The speaker may point to the flag beside the platform or to the Bible on the pulpit. He may speak of those in favor of a policy and of those against it, pointing to each group as if those people were actually present before him. In order to indicate in this manner, you may point with the finger, indicate with the whole hand, or hold the object (real or imaginary) in your hands. Usually, your eyes will follow the gesture; that is, you will look where you're pointing, even though the people or objects you are indicating are imaginary.

The second group includes the *imitative gestures.* The speaker imitates a person or a thing in order to convey certain important characteristics. A classic example is that of a speaker struggling to describe a spiral staircase. Be careful that you don't overdo the imitation. The rule is to suggest rather than to let your imitation become a complete characterization.

The third group includes the *emphatic gestures*. These are short, quick movements which lend additional force to the speaker's words. You may use the clenched fist, driven downward as though it were a hammer driving a nail; the stroke of the index finger or of the hand; or even a slight, nodding movement of the head, called the "head stroke." Gestures of this nature give emphasis because of their timing. They must have a landing place or stopping place, and your movement must hit that "stop" at the precise time that you pronounce the word you wish to emphasize. As a general rule, a speaker should also avoid any emphatic gesture—such as "pulpit pounding"—which makes noise of its own. Let the movement of the gesture serve to reinforce the sound of the voice. Emphatic gestures are also unique in that they are never followed by the speaker's eyes. With other types, the eyes follow the movement to the object indicated. When using emphatic gestures, the speaker maintains his eye contact with the audience.

The last group includes those gestures that might be called *atmospheric*. This class includes those inconspicuous movements which the audience may not consciously observe but which serve to create the desired atmosphere for what you have to say. You may take a few steps toward the audience when you desire to impress them with the importance of your remarks. You may back up a step or two, indicating that these remarks are to be treated lightly and that the audience may relax. You may clasp your hands behind your back to give a picture of quiet, serious conversation. You may even place one hand in a pocket (being careful not to rumple your clothes too much) to give a relaxed, casual appearance. These gestures could also be classified as aspects of posture or platform presence; however, they do involve movements in the course of speaking.

There are few, if any, hard-and-fast rules about gestures. The same movement, made by two different people and spoken in rhythm with different sets of words, may mean two very different things to the same audience. The speaker is a part of a total scene which the members of the audience observe throughout the speech. They see him in terms of his whole public personality—his reputation, his appearance, his voice, his message, and every bit of information about him that they have. The gestures of the speaker ought to be appropriate to the total scene of which he is a part. As an illustration of the principle, imagine the gestures that you would expect to see used by a football coach presenting his winning team to a high school football rally. Then imagine these same movements used by a minister bringing the devotional thought at a prayer breakfast! Gestures suitable for one speaker and setting will not do at all in another.

Gestures which are effective will meet the following requirements:

1. *They will appear natural, which means that they will feel natural to you as the speaker.* If you are a beginner, you may have to force yourself to use some gestures deliberately, in artificial patterns, in order to be able to move at all in front of the audience. But you must never be satisfied with planned or artificial movements. Growing confidence and frequent practice should free you to move naturally as you speak, just as you would if you were in intent conversation with another individual.

2. *They will be in harmony with the words and ideas being expressed.* If the message is forceful and dynamic, the movements should be equally powerful. Ideas which are somber and quiet should be reinforced by gestures which are few and restrained.

3. *They will be in harmony with the setting in which you speak.* A huge stage in a big auditorium calls for great, sweeping movements. A small pulpit in a restricted, narrow sanctuary requires more restraint.

4. *They will be in rhythm with your speech.* Indicative and emphatic gestures will resemble the crack of a whip. Energy is transferred through the shoulder, arm, wrist, hand, and the whip itself until the tip of the whip delivers the crack. In the same manner, the movement of a gesture should flow over your body, from the shoulder down to arm and hand, with the index finger,

fist, open hand, or whatever furnishing the "crack" of the gesture. In other words, a gesture moves toward an exact spot in time and space. If a speaker wishes to point to the flag, for instance, he will raise his arm, extend his finger, level it at the object, and then he will hold that position for an instant before he drops his hand and arm. His gesture has moved through space and time toward that precise instant when everything stops and the attention of the audience jumps from his movements to the flag itself. This instant of stopping, this whipcrack of the gesture, must be exactly timed with the words of the speaker. Perhaps he is saying, "I want you to notice *that* flag," in such a way as to contrast it with all other flags. Then his gesture must land or crack or reach its motionless position exactly as he pronounces the word "that."

5. *They will involve the use of the whole body, for no gesture can properly be regarded as a movement of hand or arm or head alone.* When you point to an object, you will probably face toward it and look directly at it. Feet, body, eyes, shoulder, arm, and hand will all participate to some degree in the gesture made by the index finger. Any large movement that a speaker makes will probably begin at the soles of his feet and move up over the entire body. Every part of the body will, to some degree, contribute to the gesture unless some part is engaged in another purposeful movement at the same time. Any movements which are purposeless, which compete with a gesture or distract from it, should be eliminated.

Each time you talk, your entire body will be speaking and not just the parts which we call the "speech mechanism." Be sure that everything contributes to the total effect, to the one message that you are struggling to convey. Your voice should not detract from your appearance or your appearance from your words. Perhaps all may be summarized in a classic piece of advice often given to speakers: Stand up to be seen, speak up to be heard, and shut up to be appreciated.

PROJECTS AND ASSIGNMENTS

Supplementary Reading in the Speech Texts

Anderson, *Training the Speaking Voice,* Ch. 3: The Production of Vocal Tone; Ch. 5: Variety and Expressiveness; Ch. 7: Developing Clearness and "Correctness" of Speech.

Sarett, *Basic Principles of Speech,* Ch. 14: Voice and Articulation; Ch. 15: The Sounds of Connected Speech; Ch. 16: Movement and Gesture.

White, *Practical Public Speaking,* Ch. 10: An Introduction to Delivery; Ch. 12: Using the Body in Delivering the Speech; Ch. 13: Using the Voice in Delivering the Speech.

Supplementary Reading in the Preaching Texts

Blackwood, *The Preparation of Sermons,* Ch. 18: The Delivery from the Pulpit.

Jones, *Principles and Practice of Preaching,* Ch. 11: Methods of Delivery; Ch. 12: Speech Mechanism.

Writing Assignment

Discuss one of the following topics:

1. Appropriate Dress for Platform or Pulpit
2. Achieving Variety in the Speaker's Voice
3. The Use of Gestures in Speaking
4. Pronunciation: Standards and Shortcomings
5. The Sounds of the English Language
6. The Relationship between the Physical Setting and the Delivery of the Speech

Speaking Assignment

Prepare and deliver a speech of not over 10 minutes in length which fulfills the following requirements:

1. It has a detailed illustration in the introduction, in the conclusion, and under each mainhead. A visual aid may be substituted for one (but only one) of these required illustrations.

2. Each mainhead statement is to be followed by some process of clarification (a restatement of the mainhead, if nothing else).

3. The detailed illustration under each mainhead is to be followed by two or more specific instances.

4. Statistical information is used twice in the speech.

5. Quotations are used twice in the speech.

These requirements may be distributed among the subheads. For example, the first subhead might be supported by the detailed illustration while the second is supported by the two specific instances. However, every subhead should be developed by some process of clarification. These are minimum requirements. Nothing except the time limit should prevent you from using any further material that is necessary. Use the visual aid at any point you wish; just remember that the visual aid will substitute for the required illustration at only one point.

Be certain that this speech exhibits all you have learned about the title, the introduction, the central idea, unified development, careful transitions, and a conclusion that achieves a real climax. In general, follow the model given below.

Title: _____

I. Introduction
   Illustration _____

II. Central Idea: _____

III. Body
   Mainhead A _____
      (Process of clarification) _____
      Illustration: _____
      Instance: _____
      Instance: _____
      Quotation: _____
      Statistics: _____
   Mainhead B _____
      (Process of clarification) _____
      Illustration: _____
      Instance: _____
      Instance: _____
      Quotation: _____

IV. Conclusion

Illustration: _____

Rehearse this speech carefully; be sure that you have all of these materials clearly in mind. Be careful to stay within the time limit. Deliver it so that your ideas will be absolutely clear to the audience.

Listening Assignment

1. In class, outline each speech, writing the central idea, mainhead statements, and subhead statements (if any are used). Under each point on the outline, list the type of speech material used by the speaker to support that point.
2. Outside of class, listen to some speaker in a formal speech situation. Note the facts about speaker, audience, time, and so on. Then summarize your reaction to his speech delivery in terms of the following items: (a) his dress and general appearance; (b) his eye contact with the audience; (c) his use of gestures; (d) his audibility; (e) his voice quality; (f) his standards of articulation and pronunciation.

8

Other Patterns for
Your Speeches

All speeches of any type or purpose are, as we have seen, constructed of two basic types of building blocks. First, they contain the ideas that the speaker or the writer is seeking to convey to his listener or reader. Second, they contain the materials, the illustrations, explanations, quotations, and visual aids, which will serve to put across or make vivid those ideas. All communications are made up of these two kinds of things.

The speaker combines these two into a single structure of unity and harmony. Thus he must limit the territory that he plans to cover. He selects and states his ideas carefully so that they all relate to the same central idea. He may even choose his speech materials so that they all relate to a basic metaphor which runs throughout the entire speech. Finally, he combines his ideas and materials into a basic plan, a design that he has selected thoughtfully, not merely by accident. Once this plan has been determined, the speaker is ready to put his outline into final form and to begin practicing his speech.

So far, our discussion has been limited to one basic plan. Invariably, you have been instructed to state the ideas first, then to follow that statement with the materials which developed the idea presented. The central idea came before the mainheads, and the mainheads came before the subheads. The material always followed the point to which it pertained. In brief, we "told them what we were going to tell them, told them, and then we told them what we had told them."

As we consider the matter of pattern or structure, however, a second possible basic design immediately presents itself. Why couldn't a speaker reverse the order of his two basic building blocks? Why couldn't he present the material for each point first, with the statement of the idea following? As we have hinted previously, he can. Each point within the speech may be reversed, with the material being presented prior to the point which this material develops. Carry this change to its logical conclusion and you have the speaker presenting his central idea last, giving the impression that he is deriving this conclusion *from* the mainheads rather than presenting a central idea which is the basis *for* the mainheads. This inverted order of speaking, with the materials coming first and the points following and with subordinate points being presented prior to main points, may be called the *indirect order*. The other pattern that we have been following, in which the points come first and the developmental material follows, would be the *direct order*. The indirect order is sometimes called "inductive." It bears a certain relationship to the method of the scientist in that it derives principles (points) from an examination of specific facts (materials). The direct order, as we noted earlier, is sometimes called "deductive" or "didactic."

If you think in terms of the simplest possible speech, these two basic orders will be easier to understand. Such a simple speech would consist of just two parts—one point and one illustration to put that point over to the audience. The direct order would require a clear statement of this point, followed by the illustration which demonstrates it. As we have seen, a speaker would be foolish to begin his speech with the statement of his central idea. An introduction would come first, catching attention and leading to that thesis statement. The speaker would also be foolish to end the speech with the illustration; he would have a more effective speech if he would only repeat the central idea a second time. Thus, the full pattern of this simple, one-point speech in the direct order would look something like this:

I. Introduction
II. Central Idea
III. Body
    Illustration
IV. Conclusion—summary

THE INDIRECT SPEECH

The indirect order would reverse the two basic parts. The speech would begin with the telling of the story. From this illustration, the speaker would derive his central idea. No real introduction would be necessary, for a good illustration, well told, should catch the attention of the audience. In this case, the story will also lead into the point, since the point is to be derived from the story. No conclusion is necessary, either, for the point itself is a summary of all that has been said. Thus the full pattern of this simple, one-point speech in the indirect order would look something like this:

I. Body
    Illustration
II. Central Idea

An example of just such a speech would be one of Aesop's fables, in which the story constitutes the body of the speech and the central idea is called the "moral."

The addition of further materials does not change the principles involved here. Often, almost all of the supporting materials for a given point can be presented before that point is revealed. Granted, a speaker will have trouble with those materials which serve to clarify the point, for it is always difficult to try to clarify something that hasn't been stated. But with the exception of the explanations, definitions, and restatements, most of the materials can be used without hesitation. The illustration is most important, for it catches attention, arouses curiosity, and doesn't necessarily give away the point being developed. A one-point speech in the indirect order using various materials might proceed something like this:

   I. Body
      Illustration
      Instance
      Instance
      Quotation
      Visual aid
  II. Central Idea

The principles involved in the one-point speech will hold good, no matter how many mainheads and subheads may be included in the speech. Suppose that your speech happens to have three mainheads. The first two are developed by means of various speech materials. The third is supported by two subheads. The pattern of your speech might look like this:

   I. Body
      Illustration
      Statistics
        Mainhead A.
      Illustration
      Instance
      Instance
        Mainhead B.
        Quotation
        Instance
          Subhead 1
        Illustration
          Subhead 2

    Mainhead C

  II. Central Idea

This outline is true to your speech in the sense that it is a complete blueprint. Every idea and piece of material is recorded at the point where it is to be used. The outline follows the order which you as the speaker intend to follow. However, it is also very confusing. For example, look at the illustration which is indicated immediately following mainhead A. We know that because of the indirect order of this speech, this illustration pertains to mainhead B. But according to all rules of outlining, this illustration ought to pertain to mainhead A under which it falls. Perhaps all outlines should be made in direct order, with a little note in the margin of some of them saying, "to be delivered in indirect order." Such a procedure would be logical but of little practical use to the speaker who likes his outlines to resemble his speeches. To solve the problem of outline confusion, we suggest the following form which is true to the speaker's thought and procedures and at the same time clear to any reader who knows the symbolism. The revised outline of your speech would look like this:

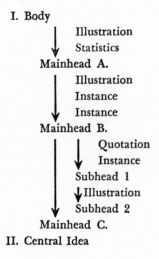

  I. Body

        Illustration

        Statistics

    Mainhead A.

        Illustration

        Instance

        Instance

    Mainhead B.

            Quotation

            Instance

        Subhead 1

        Illustration

        Subhead 2

    Mainhead C.

  II. Central Idea

The arrows should be drawn in the left margin to indicate that the direction of support has been reversed, that the points being supported *follow* the supporting material which is being presented.

Be reminded once again that the indirect order may omit both introduction and conclusion. In the outline given, the opening illustration would serve the function of the introduction. Nevertheless, it is not truly an introduction but a piece of developmental material supporting the first mainhead. The central idea, by its very nature, is a summary of the speech. Thus it may be a fine note on which to conclude. However, it still remains the central idea and not the conclusion proper. On some occasions and with certain speeches the speaker may even omit the statement of the central idea at this point, ending the speech without putting it into words. He would thus allow the listeners to infer the central idea from all that has been said.

You should not draw the conclusion from these remarks that introductions and conclusions are never used with indirect speeches. An introduction, for instance, may be needed to supply background or a setting for the speech. If such is its function, the introduction would be just as necessary with a speech in the indirect order as it would be with a speech in the direct order. Again, the conclusion is sometimes used to point out the initial steps to be taken in the course of action being advocated. If the central idea concludes that this course of action should be adopted, a conclusion may still be needed to identify these initial steps—to make your contribution or sign the commitment card or whatever. Such a conclusion would constitute the last major section of the outline and of the speech.

The chief problem in giving a speech using the indirect order is the matter of getting from one section to another. The usual techniques of transition cannot be used. A transition, you will remember, is a summary, and a summary will reveal too much of the direction that the speaker intends to follow in his indirect speech. A transition may also be regarded as a bridge. In an indirect speech, it would have to stand as a bridge with only one abutment, for the speaker does not wish to reveal the next point to which he is moving. Thus a speech in the indirect order is frequently characterized by a broken or disjointed sound in those spots where a transition would usually be employed.

There are, however, two techniques which may be used in lieu of transitions in the indirect speech. You should be familiar with both of them, for they can be your salvation in presenting a speech in this reverse order.

1. *Ask questions.* Imagine a certain hostility on the part of your audience, and ask a question which will bring that hostility out in the open and which will enable you to identify with those who are most hostile. "Does a person have to attend church in order to be a genuine Christian?" Such a question cannot be the central idea of the speech, but it can be used effectively as an introductory question to begin a discussion of the subject. "Can the experience of worship out in the forest equal the experience of worship in an ornate sanctuary?" This question would move you into a discussion of the nature of worship and its relationship to the Christian life. By raising it, you identify yourself with those members of your audience who believe that worship out in the forest *can* equal the experience of worship in a sanctuary. They cannot know that the line of thinking you are about to present is going to lead you to the conclusion (which will be your mainhead statement) that genuine Christianity involves participation in a worshiping community. This mainhead, in turn, will serve as a part of the basis for your central idea—the conclusion that assembling with God's people is one basic part of the genuine Christian life.

A common use of the question technique is in connection with what has been called the "this or nothing" procedure. It may be summarized as follows:

Introductory question: Can we follow Plan X?
Mainhead A. Plan X is not practical.

Introductory question: Can we follow Plan Y?
Mainhead B. Plan Y is psychologically unsound.
Introductory question: Can we follow Plan Z?
Mainhead C. Plan Z is beneficial in every respect.
Central Idea: We should adopt Plan Z.

In each case, the question introduces the discussion of the plan. The evidence presented then forces the conclusion which is the mainhead statement. Notice, however, that the "this or nothing" procedure rests upon the logical assumption that all possible alternatives are being considered. The listener who is aware of some other alternative has an easy escape from the speaker's argument.

2. *Tell stories.* The detailed illustration is one of the best techniques to use in moving from one division to the next when following the indirect order. The story catches attention, arouses curiosity, and moves toward the point being developed without giving it away. Sometimes the speaker will begin with a sentence such as, "The second consideration is well illustrated by the story of the. . . ." The audience will thus be aware that some new point is being introduced, without knowing what that point will be. The normal procedure, then, would be to finish the story, add the other necessary speech materials, and finally end with a clear statement of the point which has been demonstrated.

By this time, you are probably wondering why any speaker would leave the simple, direct method and try to follow this indirect order in speaking. When he does so, he obviously sacrifices some of the clarity of his speech. The clearest method is to "tell them what you're going to tell them, tell them, and tell them what you told them." Certainly, no speaker should sacrifice clarity unless he gets something in return. What does the speaker gain when he inverts his speech and uses this indirect approach?

He gains variety. Any speaker who frequently addresses the same audience should beware of the monotony of structure. The preacher on Sunday morning can easily fall into a "firstly, secondly, thirdly, brethren" sort of pattern. From time to time, he might choose to sacrifice some clarity and use the indirect method for variety's sake.

He arouses curiosity. As illustrations are recounted and other speech materials added, the audience may become curious about what the speaker has in mind. As one point follows another, people may wonder, "So what? What does all this have to do with me?" As their curiosity is aroused, they begin to listen and to become more active participants in the process of communication. The speech may not be as clear, but the audience may grasp more of it because they put more effort into the act of listening. The listeners' curiosity will be proportionate to the speaker's skill in telling his stories in an interesting manner and in concealing his points until the moment when he wants to reveal them.

He gains persuasive power. This consideration is probably the most important one in making the decision to use the indirect order. Furthermore, this persuasive power will be most effective with those who need it the most—the hostile audience.

As far as those who favor the speaker's view are concerned, an argument is an argument, no matter whether it is directly or indirectly presented. Since they accept the conclusion, they probably agree with most of the arguments supporting that conclusion. Imagine, however, the thoughts of a hostile member of the audience as he listens to a speech in the direct order. The speaker finishes his introduction and then announces: "This afternoon I want to give you some reasons why a Christian should support the efforts of those working for racial integration in our community." Immediately, the hostile listener begins to think of all of the reasons for his opposition to racial integration, and the rest of the speech is lost. The listener has identified the speaker as a member of the opposition, and a barrier has grown up between them which even the most persuasive arguments will be unable to penetrate.

On the other hand, suppose that the speaker uses the indirect order and begins by identifying himself with the members of his audience. His words may be something like this: "Many of us have been disturbed recently by the words and actions of certain strangers who have come to our community and have threatened to upset our traditions and our way of life. Nevertheless, we don't want to be in the position of opposing anything simply because it is new or upsetting; we wouldn't stand in the way of progress. As thinking people, we want to examine and evaluate; as Christians, we try to make our evaluation upon the basis of our religious faith. Therefore, this afternoon I would like to explore with you the problem of the Christian's attitude toward this whole matter of racial integration. First let us ask, are the colored races under some divine curse which the Christian is bound to respect?"

In this case, the speaker has used the question technique to define the general area he intends to explore and to move into the territory of his first mainhead. He is dealing with his subject in religious terms rather than from the standpoint of politics or economics. Therefore, he immediately confronts the main argument offered by his hostile, religious audience. His next move would be to present specific evidence leading to the conclusion that skin color, like the color of eyes or hair, is simply an accident of nature and has no basis in any divine curse.

By the time he has examined the facts and reached this first conclusion (the first mainhead of his speech), many of those in his hostile audience will have stereotyped him as a member of the NAACP, and they will refuse to listen any further. But at least they listened to this point. Some others, however, will keep their minds open through a second point and maybe a third. A few may even follow through to the conclusion, that a Christian should not oppose those forces which are breaking down racial barriers. (Such a negative position is about as far as a speaker could go in stating his central idea on this sub-

ject for a hostile audience.) Even one shifted vote in a hostile
group should be considered a major victory; a reduction in
the intensity of the hostility would make the speech worthwhile.

These principles that we have been discussing in connection
with the switching of a speech from direct to indirect order may
also apply to any point within a speech. The desire to create
variety, to arouse curiosity, or to persuade on a point where some
listeners may be hostile might lead a speaker to invert just that
one point, leaving the rest of the speech in the normal, direct
order. A speech which is only partially inverted could be called a
semi-indirect speech.

THE SEMI-INDIRECT SPEECH

The semi-indirect speech tends to fall into one of two types.
In one case, the mainheads are all left in the direct order, but
the central idea is stated at the end. In such a speech, the introduction would be necessary, but the concluding central idea
might function in place of the usual formal conclusion. The
second type of semi-indirect speech leaves the introduction and
central idea in the normal position but inverts all of the mainheads. Since the central idea is stated near the beginning, a conclusion would also be required in this type of speech order.
However, these two general types are by no means the limit of
the variations possible in the semi-indirect speech. Since any
single point or sub-point in the entire speech might be inverted,
the total number of variations possible is limited only by the
number of individual points being used in the speech.

The most important thing to remember is this: *A good speaker
never arranges his speech by accident.* He thinks through every
point, examining its logic and checking the materials which he
will use in putting it across to the audience. Then he decides—
on the basis of his need for variety, curiosity, or persuasive pow-

er as opposed to his need for clarity—the exact order in which he will present each point in the entire speech. Only then is he ready to settle on a final copy of his outline.

All speeches that have any structure or order at all may be classified in the terms that we have already considered. If each point comes first and is followed by its development, the speech fits the direct order. If the development comes first and the points are derived from the materials, the speech follows the indirect order. Any combination of the two methods may be called the semi-indirect order.

There are other speech patterns or plans, however, which seem to differ from the basic arrangements that we have listed. Actually, the differences are only apparent, not real. In each case the new pattern is simply the result of looking at the speech from a different point of view and using a different set of terms to describe the parts. Compare the two basic patterns below, and you will understand what is being done. The pattern on the left should now be familiar to you. The pattern on the right may seem strange, but closer examination will reveal that it is merely a restatement of the familiar pattern on the left.

One-point speech in direct order	*Speech seen from audience viewpoint*
I. Introduction	I. Ho-hum
II. Central Idea	II. Why bring that up?
III. Body	III. For instance?
Material to develop	Instances
the central idea	IV. So what?
IV. Conclusion	

The speech on the left is stated from the viewpoint of the speaker. That on the right is stated in terms of audience attitudes which the speaker must confront. Both outlines could represent the same speech equally well.

THE PROBLEM-SOLUTION SPEECH

A similar situation is that of the "motivated sequence" or "problem-solution" speech. It represents a psychological view of the speech structure, an attempt to carry the audience through the steps that a rational being should follow in reaching a decision or adopting a course of action. A typical outline might look like this:

I. Attention
   Method used to capture the interest of the audience
II. Problem (or need)
   A. First aspect of the problem
      Material to develop this point
   B. Second aspect of the problem
      Material to develop this point
III. Solution being advocated (or satisfaction of need)
   A. First step in solution
      Material to develop this point
   B. Second step in solution
      Material to develop this point
IV. Visualization
   An illustration or other material to make the audience visualize the advantages of the solution
V. Action proposed
   Explanation (or a series of steps) of the action to be taken by the individuals in the audience in order to put the solution into effect

The second and third parts of this problem-solution speech may become little speeches in their own right. The problem may be seen as a single thing (in which case there would be no divisions under II), or it may have two or more parts. In the same manner, the solution may be a single move (in which case there would be no divisions under III), or it may have two or more parts or steps. The last part of this speech, the action step, is usually very brief and consists of a few specific things which might be done by the audience actually present. Any of the subordinate points could also be presented in indirect order as well as in direct order.

If this problem-solution speech corresponds with one of the patterns that we have outlined earlier, which one is it? Obviously, the attention step corresponds with the usual speech introduction, and the action step with the conclusion. The visualization step is probably an expansion of the application of the solution being advocated. Whether the two main areas of problem and solution constitute an indirect or a direct speech order is a question which cannot be answered in theoretical terms; the true answer depends on the individual speech. Each message in the problem-solution pattern will have its own characteristics. One will be primarily direct, another indirect, depending on how the subject is handled.

If the problem-solution procedure overlaps the other patterns that we have discussed, why should we concern ourselves with it? Why shouldn't we think of all speeches in terms of the direct, indirect, and semi-indirect orders? If we were concerned with nothing more than taking notes on other speakers, these three basic patterns would certainly be adequate. If you organize many speeches for yourself, however, you will find this psychological method a very handy tool. You have already experienced the difficulties of wording the central idea and the mainheads of the speech. Sometimes you can avoid these problems by changing your frame of reference and thinking of the speech in terms of problem and solution. You can thereby save both time and trouble and still maintain the unity of the address. The psychological method is especially effective for use with an audience which agrees with your point of view but needs to be motivated to do something about its beliefs.

The charts which follow should help you understand the various basic speech patterns which are available for your use.

LOGICAL PATTERNS FOR SPEECH

one-point direct method

I. Introduction
II. Central Idea
III. Body
    (List of materials used)
IV. Conclusion

one-point indirect method

I. Introduction (optional)
II. Body
   ↓ (List of materials used)
III. Central Idea (may be implied)
IV. Conclusion (optional)

Direct method with mainheads

I. Introduction
II. Central Idea
III. Body
   A. Mainhead
      (List of materials)
   B. Mainhead
      1. Subhead
        (Materials)
      2. Subhead
        (Materials)
IV. Conclusion

Indirect method with mainheads

I. Introduction (optional)
II. Body
   ↓ (List of materials)
   A. Mainhead
      ↓ (Materials)
      1. Subhead
      ↓ (Materials)
      2. Subhead
   B. Mainhead
III. Central Idea (may be implied)
IV. Conclusion (optional)

Combined methods (semi-indirect)

I. Introduction
II. Central Idea
III. Body
   ↓ (List of materials)
   A. Mainhead
   ↓ (List of materials)
   B. Mainhead
IV. Conclusion

I. Introduction
II. Body
   A. Mainhead
      (List of materials)
   B. Mainhead
      (List of materials)
III. Central Idea (may be implied)
IV. Conclusion (optional)

(Any combination of the direct and indirect methods may be called semi-indirect.)

PSYCHOLOGICAL PATTERN FOR SPEECHES

I. Attention (corresponds to introduction)

II. Problem or Need
   (May have divisions or just materials to illustrate the fact of the problem)

III. Criteria for solution (optional)
   (List and explain standards which any reasonable solution may be expected to meet)

IV. Solution or Satisfaction
   (May have divisions or just materials to illustrate the one solution advocated)

V. Visualization (optional)
   (Positive—illustrates the change for the better if solution is adopted)
   (Negative—illustrates the change for the worse if solution is ignored)

VI. Action (corresponds to conclusion)
   (May have divisions listing the steps to be taken or may present materials to motivate the audience to one specific step)

PROJECTS AND ASSIGNMENTS

Supplementary Reading in the Speech Texts

McCall and Cohen, *Fundamentals of Speech,* Ch. 5: Structural Patterns.
Monroe and Ehninger, *Principles and Types of Speech,* Ch. 16: Adapting the Speech Organization to the Audience: The Motivated Sequence; Ch. 17: Making an Outline.

Supplementary Reading in the Preaching Texts

Davis, *Design for Preaching,* Ch. 9: Organic Forms; Ch. 10: Continuity: Nature and Types.
Luccock, *In the Minister's Workshop,* Ch. 13: Some Types of Outline.

Writing Assignment

Discuss one of the following topics:
1. Speech and Sermon Types: Methods of Classification
2. Using the Motivated Sequence
3. Making the Speech Pattern Fit Audience and Occasion
4. The Relationship of Speech Pattern to Subject Matter
5. Possibilities for Variety in Sermon Structure
6. The Speaker's Personality in His Choice of Speech Structure

Speaking Assignment

Prepare and deliver a speech of 5 to 7 minutes in length, using the semi-indirect order. Begin with the usual type of introduction and statement of the central idea, but present your supporting material for each mainhead before you state it. This speech may *not* be a speech for the general purposes of information or entertainment, but it must be a speech to motivate in some way. Follow this model in preparing your outline:

Title: _____

I. Introduction
   Method to be used: _____
II. Central Idea: _____
III. Body
   | Illustration: _____
   ↓ (List of other materials to be used)
   Mainhead A _____
   | Illustration: _____
   ↓ (List of other materials to be used)
   Mainhead B _____
IV. Conclusion
   Method to be used: _____

The model suggests that you use the illustration technique to move from one mainhead to the next. Don't forget that the procedure of asking questions may also prove useful. Be sure that you conceal each mainhead until you are ready to state it.

Listening Assignment

1. In class, make a complete outline of each speech, labeling each type of material used by the speaker. Listen carefully; the semi-indirect order is much more difficult to follow than the direct order which you have heard before. In addition, list the following two items for each speaker: (a) the aspect of his appearance that most needs improvement; (b) the aspect of his speech (voice and diction) that most needs improvement.

2. Outside of class, listen to some speaker in a formal speech situation. Note the facts about speaker, audience, time. Then outline his speech in full, noting the general pattern used, the points made, and the types of material used in discussing these points. Indicate in one sentence what you believe to be the single most important factor which influenced the speaker to choose the pattern which he used. Was it the subject matter, the audience, the occasion? What?

9

Your Speech Personality

Every speech, to some degree, is an attempt to motivate the audience. If your primary purpose in speaking fits the classification of "to persuade" or "to activate," these motivational aspects are obvious. However, the speech to entertain also seeks to move the audience to interest or, beyond that, to amusement or laughter. The speech to inform stimulates interest and must move the audience to appreciate the need for gaining and retaining the information.

In ancient times, the writers who discussed this subject thought of three channels through which the audience could be motivated. One of these was the channel of logic, the force of the arguments that the speaker could present to prove his viewpoint. A second was the channel of emotion, the manner in which a speaker could relate his ideas to the sympathies or feelings of his audience so that emotional responses would be set off in harmony with his cause. The third was the force of the speaker's personality itself. These were the three "modes" of persuasion.

While this classification is valuable and we intend to follow it, we also recognize certain difficulties with these three areas. The third clearly overlaps the first two. The speaker's personality will interact with any audience in complex ways that are both logical and emotional. The speaker may be logically evaluated just as any authority may be evaluated. Is he of good character? Is he honest? Can we trust his word? Is he intelligent enough to know what he is talking about? Are his intentions good; is he here to assist us in making right decisions, in contrast to some other speaker who might come to deceive or mislead? Has he really studied the subject, and is he in a position to speak with some authority? All such questions refer to the logical evaluation or the weight that should be assigned to the unsupported word of the speaker, apart from whatever supporting material he may submit to prove his case.

Audience reaction to the speaker may also be purely emotional. Perhaps he resembles the stereotype of the "good guy" that we have formed from watching western movies or television programs; so we feel he is to be trusted. Or he may bear a superficial resemblance to someone we have known and greatly admired. As a result, we may assume, without evidence or thought, that the speaker is a man of intelligence, good character, and goodwill. On the other hand, unusual hesitation in speech may produce the feeling in us that the speaker is stupid; lack of eye contact that he is dishonest; and weakness of voice that he isn't sincere in what he is saying. These positive and negative reactions are unwarranted by the facts of the case, but they all have a very real influence on the effectiveness of the speaker.

You should remember, therefore, that all aspects of yourself which we group under the heading of "personality" will have a vital effect upon the accomplishment of your speech purpose, and that this effect will exist no matter what the specific purpose may be. If the audience reaction to you is generally positive, they will be easier to interest and to amuse, more open to new information, more willing to acknowledge your arguments. If their reaction to you is generally negative, they will be eager to laugh at you but not with you, their minds will become closed and rigid, and they will refute the arguments you advance. You had better face the question now: What kind of person will the audience find you to be when you rise to speak?

Every audience will possess, to some degree, two sources of information about you. The first is your reputation—what the audience has heard about you ahead of time, before you ever stand before them. The publicity that is released for any one speech will usually be under your control and thus ought to be favorable. Other factors may not be under your control—public stands that you have taken in the past for unpopular causes, unfounded rumors that may circulate about you, unfortunate items that your enemies may bring to public attention. You would be wise to remember the ancient definition: the good speaker is the *good man speaking*. Let your life generally exhibit those qualities of intelligence, good character, and goodwill which should leave all men favorably disposed toward you.

The second source of information which the audience has about you becomes available to them when you rise to speak. Everything about you, the way you look, the way you stand, what you have to say and how you say it, will contribute to the impression of you that the audience is building up. To paraphrase an old proverb, what you seem to be may speak so loudly that the audience can't hear the message you are trying to transmit. Positive reactions will be created by sincerity, friendliness, enthusiasm, a calm sense of authority, and the apparent desire to discuss your subject in a fair and open-minded way, Negative reactions may stem from your seeming too authoritative and self-assured, insincere, too aloof and superior to the audience, unconcerned about your audience or subject matter, or from approaching the subject in a prejudiced or biased way. Your words and your manner must never convey the feeling that you know everything that is to be known on this subject. Neither should you indicate in any way that members of your audience might be stupid, prejudiced, ignorant, or inferior to you in any sense.

The speaker who flaunts his superiority alienates people, but so does the speaker who exhibits signs of his feelings of inferiority. Thus one of the greatest handicaps that the average speaker faces in trying to make a positive impression on the audience is the handicap of his own fear. If he could just be his normal, friendly self—the person that he is in his own living room or out on the golf course—he wouldn't have to worry about making a good impression.

You can probably think of a hundred social situations in which you could converse with another person fluently and confidently, words and ideas coming freely to your mind, and your only concern being that the other person won't give you the chance to say all that you have to say. But if you are moved out of those situations, placed in front of a group of people with all of their attention focused on you, and given twenty or thirty minutes of uninterrupted time in which to say what you have to say, some remarkable change takes place. Your mind turns blank, your stomach twists into a hard knot, the words won't come to your lips, your hands double in size, and your face becomes a frozen mask. The personality that you present to your audience probably approaches one of two extremes. Either you face them with all the confidence and authority of a frightened rabbit or, in the attempt to cover up the way you feel, you shout and bluster and attack imaginary opponents. Neither method is helpful in winning friends for yourself or your views.

What causes this stage fright? Some of our fears of the speech situation are so silly and groundless that they disappear as soon as we start to think about them. More reasonable causes of fear may be found among the following:

1. *The awareness of being publicly evaluated.* Most of us can play chopsticks on the piano. Suppose you were asked to play this piece in a great concert hall filled with music critics! In a similar way, all of us can talk to ourselves, but the thought of

talking before an audience that might be critical frightens us. The more expert the pianist becomes, the less he need fear the critics. The speaker also may reduce his fear by repeated successful appearances before audiences and by adequate preparation for speaking.

2. *The strangeness of the situation.* Most of us were afraid of the water when we first started to swim. One former paratrooper in a speech class remarked that his first speech was a more difficult experience than his first jump. With practice and experience in both activities, his fears of speaking and jumping were notably reduced. The act of addressing an audience may be strange, but you are already beginning to get used to it.

3. *The idea that public speaking is a peculiar, unnatural situation.* Some people think that public speaking is "putting on a show." Others believe that the speaker's hands must move only in certain ways, that an error in grammar is a disgrace, that the speaker must never hesitate while looking for a word, or that their own educational background is inadequate for them to be public speakers. By this time you should realize that all of these ideas are, at least to some degree, mistaken. Speaking to a hundred people all at once should be just as natural, and a lot more efficient, than speaking to a hundred people one at a time.

4. *The idea that you are expected to be frightened.* You can become so worried about the possibility of experiencing stage fright that your own thoughts can frighten you. This is the reason we have said nothing about stage fright earlier in this study. The more you think about being frightened, the more frightened you may become. Therefore, we have tried to help you concentrate on the importance of the message you have to convey, hoping you will forget to be afraid.

The man who runs through a burning hotel, pounding on doors and shouting to awaken the sleepers, may be frightened by the fire, but he probably doesn't experience stage fright. He wastes no time worrying about his voice quality, his choice of language, or the precise spot that his knuckles must touch each door. His message has become so vital to him and to his hearers that the techniques of communication are forgotten in the overwhelming need to accomplish his purpose. He has stumbled on the secret of confidence in speaking. You can't overcome your fear of anything simply by working at not being afraid. Confidence comes from an overpowering sense of mission which subordinates everything else in your consciousness.

How can you overcome your fear of speaking? Perhaps you are disappointed at this point that you still experience stage fright at all. You thought that a speech book would solve this problem for you in three easy lessons, and now you find that the trembling knees are still with you. Is there something abnormal about your reactions? No, your feelings are about the same as those of most good speakers—even of politicians in the middle of a campaign or ministers who occupy the pulpit twice every Sunday. You may receive some help, however, if you remember these considerations:

1. *A certain amount of tension before an audience is to be desired.* Fear releases glandular secretions into the blood stream to give you powers you do not ordinarily possess. You become more alert and more emotionally responsive. Your muscle tone will be improved. Your enthusiasm and vitality will become more pronounced and more obvious and will thus have a greater effect upon the audience. Most good speakers come to enjoy this feeling of exhilaration in somewhat the same manner that people enjoy the thrill of riding a roller coaster in an amusement park.

2. *Fear of an audience is common to most speakers.* In fact, the experience is familiar to singers, actors, and almost all who engage in some form of public performance. If you are afraid when you stand up to speak, you have lots of company.

3. *The audience need never know you are nervous.* Fear cannot be seen; it is a feeling, not an object to be observed. What the audience does observe are the little signs which may result from this fear—the purposeless movements, the lack of fluency in

the speech. If the speaker can control these signs, the audience will never discover how frightened he feels.

4. *Enthusiasm for the message overcomes fear.* Always choose the subject or topic that means the most to you. Then, as the old saying goes, "Open your mouth and throw yourself into it." Think in terms of your audience. Remember how important your ideas are for them, how vital to their lives. Lose yourself in your message.

5. *Work for self-mastery.* The speaker must be able to take charge of the situation in which he speaks. Anything can happen when you are in front of an audience. Your mind can go blank. You may say something you never intended. The audience may laugh at you. Some unfortunate thing over which you have no control may take place. Events such as these put you to the test and reveal the depth of your inner resources. No minister should stand in the pulpit unless he feels the support of a greater Power than his own helping him to control himself and the situation.

6. *The best safeguard against fear is careful preparation.* Assemble more material than you can possibly use. Select the best and put it into the proper order. Plan the outline thoughtfully, so that the structure is logical. Then practice the speech out loud several times, both with and without reference to your prepared outline. Have the first and last sentences clearly in mind, but make no attempt to memorize the entire speech. Remember that proper preparation is spiritual as well as intellectual.

7. *Relax before you get up to speak.* Interest yourself in the situation, the auditorium, the audience, or the words of the previous speaker. Take a few deep breaths. Relax physically by tensing a group of muscles and then relaxing, getting rid of the tense feeling. Don't think about your speech. If your preparation has been adequate, the ideas will come to you at the proper time.

8. *Get hold of yourself before you start to speak.* When you stand before the audience, pause, look directly at them, and

take charge of the situation. Don't rush like a frightened boy who starts to run as he passes a graveyard. Take the time to control both your audience and yourself.

9. *Think of your speech as an enlarged conversation,* not as some peculiar kind of show. You are talking to individuals, just as you might talk to them in your living room.

10. *Try to appear confident.* Stand straight and tall; look the members of the audience directly in the eye. People take you at your own estimate. Moreover, if you act as though you are confident, you will soon find that you become confident.

11. *Be physically active.* Avoid little, nervous movements such as rattling the keys or the change in your pockets, but use lots of large, purposeful movements. Don't be afraid to walk about when the moving is meaningful in relation to your speech. Talk with your hands.

12. *Don't be rigid in following the speech that you planned.* If the right word won't come to mind, use the best word you can. If you forget that valuable illustration, skip it and go to the next point. If you forget the next division, move on to whatever division you can remember. Many times you will be able to remember those points or illustrations and weave them into the speech later on. If your mind goes completely blank, summarize. That process may renew your train of thought so that you can go on. If it doesn't, a summary makes a good conclusion, and no one may be the wiser. Above all, don't stop. In the words of a famous preacher, the important thing is to "keep the blessed sound a-going."

13. *Don't be afraid to let the audience laugh at you.* If you forget or make a mistake, confess what you have done and let them enjoy a laugh at your expense. The sympathy that you win may more than compensate for your error.

These practical bits of advice should not draw your attention away from your ultimate goal as a speaker. Try to become, in actuality, the "good man speaking." Don't be satisfied merely to *seem* good to the members of your immediate audience. Even

Hitler could do as much. Examine yourself apart from the speech situation. As a human being, how *good* are you, really?

Can you measure up to the moral standards of your community? We do not expect speakers to be saints merely because they are speakers. We do expect you to tell the truth without undue exaggeration, to champion the weak, the old and feeble, the young and helpless. We want to see evidence that you try to do to others as you would have them do to you. We expect you to show some respect for our country and its laws.

Are you intelligent, at least in the subject area that you are discussing? Do you hold a viewpoint with some responsible basis, and does your support of that viewpoint also involve an appeal to our intelligence? We expect you to have feelings and convictions, of course. We want you to take a side and advocate it to the best of your ability. However, we feel that you should start from reasonable and clear assumptions and move to the conclusions with due regard for logical processes.

Are you a person of goodwill? It is not enough for you to want what is "best" for us according to your definition. You must also treat us as humans with freedom of choice, not as objects to be manipulated. You must not persuade us by psychological techniques so that we will make a decision today under the influence of your powerful oratory and regret it tomorrow when we view it in the light of reason. Both your motives and your methods must regard us as ends in ourselves, never as means to some end of your own.

These few ideas are not intended as a code of ethics for speakers; as such, they would accomplish little. The evil man, secure in his own pride, would never notice his own violations of the code. The saint, overly conscientious, would be discouraged from speaking at all. Besides, who among us has the right to set up a code of goodness? We discuss the subject here in the hope that your self-examination will lead to growth in this aspect of speaking, just as you are growing in other aspects.

PROJECTS AND ASSIGNMENTS

Supplementary Reading in the Speech Texts

Aristotle, *The Rhetoric,* Book II, Ch. 1.

Brigance, *Speech: Its Techniques and Disciplines in a Free Society,* Ch. 4: First Steps in Managing Yourself; Ch. 19: Ethical Persuasion.

Dickens, *Speech: Dynamic Communication,* Ch. 2: Gaining Confidence and Poise; Ch. 18: The Speaker's Personality; Ch. 19: The Speaker's Ethical Responsibility.

Supplementary Reading in the Preaching Texts

Brooks, *Lectures on Preaching,* Ch. 2: The Preacher Himself; Ch. 3: The Preacher in His Work.

Forsyth, *Positive Preaching and Modern Mind,* Ch. 2: The Authority of the Preacher.

Kennedy, *His Word Through Preaching,* Ch. 5: As One Having Authority; Ch. 6: After I Have Preached to Others.

Writing Assignment

Discuss one of the following topics:
1. The Causes and Cures of Stage Fright
2. The Persuasive Power of the Personality
3. The Bases of Personal Appeal in Speaking
4. The Personality as a Factor in Preaching
5. The Preacher's Sense of Authority
6. Making the Good Speaker Truly Good

Speaking Assignment

Prepare a speech of 5 to 7 minutes in length using the pure indirect or inductive order. Present the materials before stating each mainhead, and leave the central idea until all of the mainheads have been presented. You may not need an introduction or conclusion. This speech may *not* be a speech to inform but must be for some other general purpose. Model your speech after this pattern:

Title: _____

I. Introduction (optional)
   Method to be used _____
II. Body
   | Illustration _____
   ↓   (List other materials to be used)
   Mainhead A _____
   | Illustration _____
   ↓ (List other materials)
   1. _____
   | Illustration _____
   ↓   (List other materials)
   2. _____
   Mainhead B _____
   | Illustration _____
   ↓   (List other materials to be used)
   Mainhead C _____
III. Central Idea _____
IV. Conclusion (optional)
   Method to be used _____

Listening Assignment

1. In class, fill in a small slip of paper with the following items for each speech: (a) the speaker's name; (b) mainheads of the speech, as you understood them; (c) central idea of the speech, as you understood it; (d) a suggestion for the speaker's improvement—his most noticeable weakness. Pass this criticism slip to the speaker as he finishes his speech.

2. Outside of class, listen to some speaker in a formal speech situation. Note the facts about speaker, audience, time. Then outline the speech, getting the central idea and main points. Write a one-sentence evaluation of this speaker as a person, indicating whether his personality contributed to or detracted from his speech and the reason for this judgment. Be aware of the sources of the information you had about the speaker's personality. Did you form your ideas of him solely from your observations during the speech, or did you have prior information?

10

Your Power to Persuade

We have examined the personality of the speaker as a factor in the motivation of the audience. Next, let us turn to the speech itself. If every speech seeks to motivate the audience to some degree, the persuasive aspects of the speech must never be far from the speaker's mind. These matters will be particularly important when the primary purpose of the speech is to convince, to persuade, or to activate. The successful speaker will be thinking in terms of persuasive power as he finds and selects material, as he arranges that material in order, as he chooses the words to express his ideas, and as he delivers the speech to his audience.

The ancient procedure was to classify these aspects of persuasion in terms of their logical or emotional nature. Any attempt to move the audience by means of intellect or thought processes was logical; any appeal to the feelings was emotional. Today we recognize that the division is not so simple. Logical argument can be used to support a position which is held emotionally, by a process called "rationalization." On the other hand, the assumptions which underlie a logical argument may be beyond rational proof and primarily based upon emotion. A perfectly logical argument may be effective, not because of its logic but because the use of such an argument creates the feeling that the speaker is particularly intelligent. When all is said and done, no human being acts solely on the basis of reason in all situations. If he did, he would not be human; he would be some sort of computer. Nevertheless, the analysis of the persuasive aspects of the speech on the basis of the logical and the emotional modes of persuasion may increase your understanding and implement your ability to motivate an audience.

LOGICAL PERSUASION

Logical persuasion may be viewed from two elementary positions, those of *inductive* or *deductive logic.* Inductive, or scientific, logic is of primary concern to a speaker who is selecting the materials that he will use to prove any one point, since this procedure moves from specific bits of information to a generalization that covers them. The process goes something like this: A scientist makes an observation—an apple falls off a tree and strikes Newton on the head. He combines this scientific fact with many similar observations—many apples have been seen to fall off trees, and they all moved downward toward the center of the earth. Other objects, such as pears and peaches and stones and books, seem to follow the same course when released. On the basis of all of these specific observations, the scientist creates a hypothesis—some kind of a generalization or law (in this case, a law of gravity) which will state the basic principle of behavior which seems to underlie all of the specific cases. Since scientists like to be very careful about such things, our scientist will now devise some additional, specific situation in which another observation can be made under controlled conditions. If this observation agrees with the others and if continued experiments yield the same results, his hypothesis will become a "law."

In a similar manner, a speaker assembles "observations" pertaining to the subject which concerns him. These specific cases are the speech materials. He may describe in detail some automobile accident in which speed was a primary factor. He may then list additional cases of a similar nature. He may add the observations of qualified witnesses giving their conclusions that speed has been a factor in many past accidents. All of these facts point to one conclusion: excessive speed causes automobile accidents. This hypothesis could constitute one of the points in a speech; the speaker established it by means of inductive reasoning. Furthermore, the reasoning process is the same, whether the speaker announces his point first and then presents the evidence or presents the supporting materials first followed by the point.

Inductive reasoning is always open to error, even when used by the most carefully trained scientist. Was the original observation a "scientific fact" in the sense of being a careful, objective recording of an event that actually took place? Was the scientist fooled by a mirage? Do several senses or several observers combine to corroborate the data? Can the experience of an observer be explained in some other way? Did he see a flying saucer or only a glowing cloud of marsh gas? How many observations are necessary before one is entitled to formulate a hypothesis or to consider his hypothesis to be a law? What about contradictory events, those facts which seem to preclude the hypothesis being advanced?

Even the best conclusions of inductive reasoning are always a bit tentative and uncertain. The fact that all of the apples in history have fallen off trees and gone toward the center of the earth really proves with certainty nothing about the next apple that might happen to fall from a tree. Besides, a speaker uses his specific cases to support generalizations of much less certainty than the law of gravity. He assembles evidence to establish the probability of a point. At the same time, he recognizes that an opponent might assemble another collection of specific examples to demonstrate the truth of a contradictory point. The speaker who persuades his audience by inductive reasoning is the one who presents sufficient evidence to make his generalizations seem most probable.

Deductive reasoning proceeds in a different direction. It begins with a generalization and utilizes that principle to draw a conclusion about a specific case. The classic example looks like this:

> All men are mortal.
> Socrates is a man.
> Therefore, Socrates is mortal.

In this case, two general facts are assumed to be true: all men are mortal, and Socrates is a man. On the basis of these two principles, you are entitled to draw a specific conclusion, that Socrates is mortal. If your generalizations are true and if the reasoning used in arriving at the conclusion is valid, the specific conclusion is absolutely certain. Socrates really is mortal.

Thinkers are rarely certain about the truth of these generalizations or "premises" because these principles usually are derived from some process of inductive reasoning. We have already seen that inductive reasoning gives only a degree of probability, never absolute certainty, about a conclusion. The thinker must also be careful of the validity of his deductive reasoning, for fallacies in reasoning are common. We can easily create another simple syllogism to show how easy it is to fall into a trap. Notice how similar this argument seems to be to the one already stated.

> All fish can swim.
> Henry can swim.
> Therefore, Henry is a fish.

In this case, the premises of the argument are perfectly true. All fish can swim, and Henry can swim. But Henry happens to be an intelligent human being, not a fish. Something has gone wrong with the reasoning process.

The precise nature of these fallacies need not concern us here. You will find them discussed in detail in some of the additional readings listed at the end of this chapter. Our problem as speakers is to demonstrate a high degree of probability in the points that we make. Then we must combine these in an argument that is logically sound. The demonstration of probability is chiefly inductive logic. The combination of points in a speech to persuade is most frequently a function of deductive logic.

As a speaker, you will rarely use that capsule form of deductive logic called the "syllogism," which we used in the argument about Socrates. The argument used in public speaking is so different that it is sometimes given a different name. In ancient times Aristotle called the speaker's type of argument the "enthymeme." Its principles, however, will be those of any deductive argument.

Take, for example, an argument as a speaker might make it:

Central Idea: You should be an active church member.
  A. Because church members contribute to their community.
  1. Because church members have high moral standards.

Now translate this line of argument into the syllogistic structure on which it rests, and you will be able to examine the speaker's logic:

All people who have high moral standards contribute to their community.
All church members have high moral standards.
All church members contribute to their community.

You should participate in anything which contributes to your community.
All church members contribute to your community.
You should be an active (participating) church member.

When the speaker's reasoning is placed in this form, it becomes easy to understand and to criticize. Is he really trying to support the term "all" in the first syllogism? Perhaps he should

be satisfied to say "some" or "most." What does he mean by
such terms as "contribute," "high moral standards," and "participate"?

The most important thing to notice, however, is the way in
which the standard syllogism has changed when it becomes part
of the structure of a speech. In each step, the first part of the
argument has been assumed. When the speaker moves from the
high moral standards of the church member to the contribution
that church members make to their communities, he assumes that
people who have such moral standards are making such a contribution. In the same manner, when he moves from the premise
that church members contribute to the community to the conclusion that you should be an active church member, he assumes that you should be active in anything that contributes
to the community.

Some of these assumptions are difficult to prove, if you stop
to question them. For instance, who could hope to participate
in everything that contributes to the welfare of any given community? One person can do only so many things! The speaker,
then, will have to add additional arguments to his subdivision on
moral standards. A second subdivision might be that church
members believe in law and order. A third subdivision might
argue that church members help the poor and needy. A fourth
subdivision could contend that church members contribute
to racial understanding. In all of these cases, the basic argument
remains unchanged. Thus,

All people who _____ contribute to their community.
All church members are people who _____.
All church members contribute to their community.

The speaker hopes that by increasing the number of these arguments, he is increasing the size and importance of the contribution which church members apparently make to the community. Thus he increases the force of his primary argument:
Since church members contribute *so much* to their community,

theirs is the type of contribution most worthy of your time and energy. These contentions give the speech its logical force and persuasive power.

When you speak, then, observe the principles of inductive reasoning in presenting your speech materials. Check your speech mainheads and subheads by the principles of deductive reasoning. But an effective speaker never forgets that the people in front of him are human beings. They cannot be expected to judge a case and to reach a decision on the basis of logical factors alone. We might wish that audiences were a bit more intelligent and thought more carefully before reaching a decision, but none of us would really want to see human feelings and emotions eliminated. We talk to real people, not thinking machines, and we should plan every aspect of the speech with that fact in mind.

EMOTIONAL PERSUASION

The most logical arguments cannot escape an appeal to human emotions. Return, for a moment, to the argument encouraging people to be active church members. Notice the language used. Expressions such as "high moral standards" and "contribute to their community" contain strong emotional appeals in themselves. How would you define "high moral standards"? Does this term refer to those who would not cheat except on their income tax or to those who would not steal unless the sum involved is less than five dollars? Do high moral standards require moral perfection? As soon as we try for a precise meaning of the term, its whole feeling seems to disappear. The language was emotional to begin with. Analysis destroys the emotion and changes the meaning.

Move beyond the language and take a look at the argument itself. We listed four things which church members "contribute to the community"—their high moral standards, their belief in law and order, their help to the poor and needy, and their contribution to racial understanding. These are only four of many genuine contributions which could be listed. With equal accuracy we could point out that Christians reduce the sales of alcoholic beverages; they encourage the creation of racially mixed neighborhoods; they keep dragging religion into the discussion of political problems; they discourage many forms of gambling. We have now listed a total of eight "contributions" made by Christians to the community. Of these, the speaker selected four. Why did he choose those four and omit the others?

The answer lies in the emotional factors which must underlie all argument. Notice the "contributions" which the speaker did not use. The sale of alcoholic beverages affects a number of people in most communities; the grocery store which does not sell beer is rare in many states. Racially mixed neighborhoods have been the subject of much controversy, perhaps even more in the North than in the South. Many people object to the pronouncements of religious groups on political issues. Gambling in some form is a part of the lives of many people and a major source of income in some states. In brief, these arguments would have little persuasive effect on an average American audience. The speaker, therefore, did not use them.

The arguments that he did use were based on the assumption that most Americans believe in high moral standards, respect law and order, sympathize with the poor and needy, and want to improve racial understanding. These viewpoints, in turn, are derived from certain basic motives which are emotional in nature. Our morality is related to our feelings about the family. Respect for law and order is related to patriotism and to self-preservation, as is our desire for racial understanding. We have a natural tendency to identify with others who may be in want or in pain. The speaker selected arguments which would appeal to these emotions.

You will find no difficulty in locating lists of the motives that impel people. Some of them are directed toward the self—health and physical well-being, self-preservation, the desire to possess power, wealth, reputation, and self-respect. Others—such as the welfare of one's family, community, nation, or religious group— are directed toward more altruistic ends. All of these motives or drives are part of our emotional orientation toward our existence. Changing a person's mind does not mean going counter to these feelings. As we have seen, the speaker selects certain drives and emphasizes them in order to overcome the opposition of other drives which might run contrary to the position he is advocating. An army officer sending his men into battle might emphasize patriotism, duty, reputation, and love of home, friends, and family, in order to overcome the drive of self-preservation which might cause his men to run instead of advancing into enemy fire. Then the speaker relates his arguments to these basic drives.

If you would be an effective speaker, remember the emotions of the audience. Keep them in mind, first, as you plan the structure of the speech and select the arguments you intend to use. As we have already noted, an expected emotional hostility toward your point of view on the part of the audience might cause you to delay the central idea and to proceed according to the indirect pattern of speech development. Your analysis of their emotions will also indicate the arguments that you should use and the arguments that you should avoid. A minister might recognize that his congregation has strong feelings about the Bible. They regard it as a holy book, the very Word of God. Thus the minister could present a very persuasive argument that a certain thing should be done "because the Bible says so." If he knows that his audience lacks these feelings and regards the Bible as just another book, he omits this argument. Even though the argument may be true, it has no persuasive force with this audience.

Remember the emotions of your audience as you choose the supporting material which will put across your ideas. Be careful as you clarify your point that you don't attack the self-respect of the hearers. Restate or explain your idea a bit too much, and you are guilty of talking down to your audience and thus insulting them as ignorant or childlike. When you verify an idea, try to get your hearers emotionally involved. Give enough detail in regard to sense perceptions and feelings so that your hearers will become participants in the story themselves. When using comparison or contrast, remember the emotional values. Compare with something which arouses pleasant feelings; contrast with that which is ugly and displeasing.

The process of amplification involves emotions also. The authority whom you quote will have a greater persuasive effect on your audience if they know him, respect him, and regard him as a sort of hero. Statistics will mean more if they are stated in human terms and represented in a manner that can be apprehended by the senses.

The application of a point should be the most emotionally powerful stage of its development. You might warn people of specific dangers involved in the decision they are about to make —dangers to life, health, or reputation. All sorts of rewards may honestly be offered them, such as improved health or financial security or increased status. All of these things can be related to the action proposed on the specific point under discussion. The emotional aspect of application may also become a powerful temptation for the orator to misuse his skill. Some speakers will warn of every conceivable danger and offer every desirable reward, whether these things are really related to the case at hand or not. Such an attempt to play upon the emotions of the audience is dishonest and self-defeating. However, the speaker who warns of genuine dangers and points out the true rewards to his hearers is not only persuasive but sincere and honest in the bargain.

The act of wording the speech also requires consideration of the emotions of the audience. Avoid the weak, the hesitant, the apologetic. On the other hand, you should also avoid the bombastic or egotistic. Imagine that you are invited to a strange home for dinner. Whether the food is well prepared or not, you will naturally find something about it that you can sincerely praise. You may hate pumpkin pie, but you pick out the virtues of this *particular* pumpkin pie. When the host's children climb all over you, you remark about their health and good spirits. If they sit listlessly in the corner, you talk about their good behavior. In a similar manner, each time you speak, you are the guest of those who come to listen. Look for opportunities to pay a sincere compliment, to offer sincere praise. You do not need to flatter. Cultivate a real love and respect for people and then let your words exhibit your genuine feelings.

Finally, the whole sweep and movement of the speech should be designed with the emotions of the audience in mind. Rhetoricians sometimes argue about whether the strong point in a speech should come first or last. The argument has little point. The fact is that every speech should have a feeling of gathering strength and power about it as it moves along; it must sweep the audience before it as it goes, must "catch fire" before the end. This movement is not a matter of increased speed or volume in delivery, although some speakers try to get results by such mechanical means. Rather, the emotional force of the speech should increase as the speech progresses.

In this sense, the introduction to a speech may actually be too good. Perhaps you have heard a speaker who began in such a gripping way that the sheer drama of his words held the audience spellbound for a time; then the speech went downhill and fell apart before the conclusion. The introduction was such a good one that the rest of the speech couldn't live up to it. In such a case, the speaker might be wise to take the material out of the introduction and use it in the conclusion. We hate to think of any part of any speech as being *too* good. Still, the emotional peak of a speech should be reached at or near the end and not earlier.

The accomplishment of this movement in a speech may be partly a function of delivery which gains in feeling and intensity as the speaker nears the conclusion. It may also stem from the material which the speaker selects. Value the good illustration that has real emotional impact and happens to fit the conclusion of your speech. The feeling of movement may also be gained from the arrangement of ideas in the speech. Note the following outlines:

> *Central Idea:* The Christian life is one of constant growth. Let us examine the four great areas in which this growth should take place.
> A. The Christian grows intellectually.
> B. The Christian grows physically.
> C. The Christian grows spiritually.
> D. The Christian grows socially.

The basis of this message should be familiar to you; it is found in Luke 2:52 where these areas of growth are ascribed to Jesus. The order used, unfortunately, is the order of the text. Notice what happens when this order is changed so that the speech rises in emotional power:

> *Central Idea:* Let us examine the four great areas of Christian growth.
> A. The Christian grows physically.
> B. The Christian grows intellectually.
> C. The Christian grows socially.
> D. The Christian grows spiritually.

Movement of this type gives the speech emotional power and makes it truly persuasive. It marks the difference between mere talking and great speaking.

PROJECTS AND ASSIGNMENTS

Supplementary Reading in the Speech Texts

Abernathy, *The Advocate,* Ch. 4: Appeal to Reason—Inductive; Ch. 5: Appeal to Reason—Deductive; Ch. 7: Appeal to Emotions.

Aristotle, *The Rhetoric,* Book I, Chs. 1-2.

Walter, *Speaking to Inform and Persuade,* Ch. 5: Persuasion: An Overview; Ch. 6: Persuasive Logic: The Tactics of Persuasion; Ch. 7: Emotion and Motivation: The Strategy of Persuasion.

Supplementary Reading in the Preaching Texts

Garrison, *The Preacher and His Audience,* Ch. 10: Emotional Factors in Persuasion.

Weatherspoon, *Sent Forth to Preach,* Ch. 5: Making Disciples.

Writing Assignment

Discuss one of the following topics:

1. The Relative Importance of Logical, Emotional, and Personal Persuasion
2. Avoiding Logical Fallacies
3. The Place of Persuasion in Preaching
4. Persuasion as Distinct from Manipulation
5. Persuasiveness as a Factor in Evaluating Speech Materials
6. Persuasiveness as a Factor in Planning Speech Structure

Speaking Assignment

Prepare and deliver a speech of 5 to 7 minutes in length on a subject of your own choosing. This speech should meet the following requirements:

1. It should be a speech not to inform or to entertain but to motivate in some way.

2. It must be organized according to the problem-solution or motivated-sequence pattern. The four steps—attention, problem, solution, and action—are required. The other two steps—criteria for solution and visualization—may be used or omitted as you wish.

3. It should generally conform to the following pattern:

Title: _____

I. Attention step
   Method to be used: _____

II. Problem
   (May be single, or may be divided into several aspects)
III. Criteria for solution (optional)
   (Here, you would list several standards which any reasonable solution should meet.)
IV. Solution
   (May be single, or may be divided into several aspects)
V. Visualization (optional)
   Method: _____
VI. Action
   (Must be specific. May be single, or may be divided into several steps.)

Listening Assignment

1. In class, write a brief criticism sheet for each speaker. Include the following two items: (a) his greatest strength as a speaker (be specific) ; (b) his greatest weakness as a speaker (be specific) . Pass the appropriate criticism sheet to each speaker at the end of the class hour.
2. Outside of class, listen to some speaker in a formal speech situation, keeping a record of the speaker, audience, occasion. Outline the speech briefly, getting the central idea and main points. Write a one-paragraph criticism of the logic of the speech, evaluating both the structure of the speech and the materials used in this respect.

11
Using the Right Word

In ancient times the study of public speaking was divided into five areas. The first of these was *invention,* the process of creating the ideas and assembling the materials of the speech. The second was *disposition* or arrangement, the organization of the speech into some sort of order. Another area was *delivery,* the pronunciation of the words for the ears of the audience. Another was *memory,* the ability of the speaker to remember the words and ideas to be presented.

You will recognize that our study so far has included all four of these areas to some degree. We have spent a great deal of time on invention and disposition. We devoted one chapter to delivery. We have not emphasized memory as such, but we have insisted that the speech structure be simple, clear, and easy for both speaker and listener to remember.

We now turn to the fifth of the ancient areas, speech *style,* a subject that has not directly concerned us before this point. We use the word "style" with its ancient meaning, the expression of thought in words. Some modern authors give the term a broader denotation, using it to refer to mannerisms of delivery or to any peculiarly individual aspects of speaking. In contrast, we shall use the word "style" to mean the clothing of thought in language.

The study of style would make a profitable full-time occupation for the man who would speak well, an occupation that could keep him busy for life. No speaker or writer ever reaches the place where the choice of a word, the turn of a phrase, or the order of a sentence cannot be improved. New figures of speech may be invented which are so striking that they are quoted and repeated until they finally cease to be figures and become part of the language itself. A discussion of the principles of style would take too much space here, and you will have no trouble in finding authors to guide you. Let us list only a few of the important considerations in order to call them to your immediate attention.

Seek the right word. Choose the word that conveys the exact shade of meaning you want to express. One word is not as good as another. Compare the following expressions:

> Since I enjoy a relationship with God which is roughly analogous to that between a sheep and its shepherd, I have an inner assurance that all my basic and primary needs will receive satisfaction.

> The Lord is my shepherd; I shall not want.

The ideas conveyed are approximately the same. The second sentence says them much more effectively, in part because the words chosen are exactly right.

Seek the "correct" word. Choose the grammatically proper expression. The rules of grammar were not passed by some legislative body in order to create problems for public speakers. Rather, they are based upon our need to communicate our thoughts clearly and accurately. Notice how the following errors create confusion and misunderstanding:

"Everyone are coming to the party." The words "everyone" and "are" contradict each other. Which did the speaker intend?

"He didn't want no apples." Does the negative "didn't" apply to the "no" or to the "apples"? Did he want apples or not?

"Returning from the far country, the father welcomed the prodigal son." Who had been in that far country, the father or the son?

In other cases, the rules of grammar may have little to do with understanding. They are more like rules of etiquette. You can eat potatoes with your knife if you try, but it isn't done in polite society. Like rules of etiquette, the rules of grammar had better be observed if you want to be accepted in good company.

However, do not let these remarks lead you to an exaggerated idea of the importance of correct grammar. Even well-educated people, when not delivering a speech from memory or reading it from manuscript, will occasionally make technical errors. For instance, you may begin a sentence with "who" and then conclude it in such a way that the original "who" should have been "whom." By the time you discover your error, the sentence is half spoken, and it is too late for you to return to correct the initial interrogative. Such mistakes are not serious. Purists love to tell us that we should not split infinitives, begin sentences with conjunctions, or end them with prepositions. These rules are doubtful for the writer and almost meaningless for the speaker. They represent pedantry "up with which we will not put." Nevertheless, you can still profit by a quick review of the proper manner of using such verbs as sit, set and lie, lay.

Seek clarity and simplicity. Use a plain style in contrast to an ornate style. Don't concern yourself about creating great literature for posterity. Give your attention to the audience before you at the moment. As someone has said, shooting over the heads of your audience doesn't prove you have good ammunition; it proves you have poor aim!

Choose simple, easy words of one syllable. A spade is a spade, not a digging implement. Naturally, you want to choose words to convey your thoughts and feelings accurately. However, you will usually find that simple, common words will do the job. Don't try to impress people with the size of your vocabulary, or you may find them completely ignorant of your message. If you are forced to use a technical vocabulary, such as the specialized language of theology, be sure to explain your terms in words people can understand.

Keep your sentences short and simple. The normal order is subject, action verb, object. Beware of the prepositional phrase and of the subordinate clause. Avoid passive verbs and linking verbs as much as possible. Don't use an adjective when you can use a verb. If you want to describe a tree in autumn, refer to it as "flaming," not merely "red."

In recent years many scholars have studied the problem of what makes written material readable. The principles involved would seem to be the same for speech as for reading. The results of these studies indicate that a writer or speaker should:

1. *Use short sentences.* The smaller the number of words used in an average sentence, the easier it is to understand the material.

2. *Use short words.* Avoid prefixes and suffixes. The smaller the average number of syllables per word, the easier it is to understand the material.

3. *Use simple sentences.* The greater the number of qualifying phrases and clauses, the more difficult it will be to understand the material.

Choose appropriate language—appropriate to the subject matter, the audience, and the occasion. The language of the locker room may be all right in the locker room; it is not appropriate to the classroom or the public auditorium. Slang may be effectively used by a teen-ager talking to his fellows at a football game; it is not in order for the minister talking to his congregation on Sunday morning. Never yield to the temptation to attract attention by using language which is extreme, out of place, or profane. The attention you attract will not be favorable.

Evaluate your language by asking yourself four basic questions. First, is it appropriate for you? A young person is expected to use more informal expressions. An older person saying the same things in the same way might sound ridiculous. The language should fit the speaker. Second, is it appropriate to the occasion? Contrast a minister's talk at a funeral with that of a coach to his football team at half time. The speaker's choice of words should vary with the situation. Third, is the language appropriate to the audience? Such differences as age, sex, intellectual level, and size will require variations in style. Finally, is the language appropriate to the subject being discussed? A serious religious talk will require a more elevated style than a repetition of the latest funny story.

Every speaker, like every writer, has a style all his own. Our chief concern should be to improve the style that is ours, to learn to express our ideas more clearly and more forcefully. Such improvement in expression does not come from memorizing rules. Practice is most important; careful, thoughtful, intelligent practice improves style. Oral practice is of some profit, but the words usually pass so quickly that we are unable to examine them and improve our choices. One could record, listen, and evaluate, but the process would be time-consuming. The best way to improve style is to write.

This fact does not contradict the general principle that beginning speakers should not write their speeches. They have not yet developed an oral style in contrast to a written style, and their speeches, if written, would "smell of the lamp." They easily fall into the temptation to make the act of speaking a memory exercise instead of an act of genuine communication. If you have been following the assignments given here, however, your situation is now quite different. You may find the following suggestions very profitable to your future growth as a speaker:

1. Occasionally write out a speech in full. Think of it, not as a

composition but as a speech. Write roughly and rapidly, just the way you talk. You can go back and polish your manuscript later. Prepare your speech carefully, practice it out loud, then (and only then) write it down in full.

2. Try writing a speech *after* you have delivered it. Remember as exactly as you can the way you phrased the ideas and put these words on paper. Then go back and try to improve the manuscript. If you have access to recording equipment, record your delivery of the speech, have the recording transcribed, and then polish your phrasing.

3. Write other things besides speeches. Rewrite some of the written assignments you have done in connection with this course of study.

4. Write letters to your friends. You will give many of them a pleasant surprise at hearing from you. A brief account of your current doings might renew the friendship.

5. Take a paragraph from a favorite book and try to rewrite it in your own words. Take a section from the work of one author and try to rewrite it in the style of another writer.

6. Keep a diary, a detailed written account of the events of each day or of each week. Such a record could be very valuable to you in the future, and the regular practice will do much to develop you as a writer.

7. Write descriptions of places you have seen.

8. Write character sketches of your friends.

9. Write poetry, even if it's bad poetry.

10. Keep on writing!

PROJECTS AND ASSIGNMENTS

Supplementary Reading in the Speech Texts

Blankenship and Wilhoit, *Selected Readings in Public Speaking,* Ch. 4: Language and Style.

Gray and Braden, *Public Speaking: Principles and Practice,* Ch. 25:

Using Language for Clarity; Ch. 26: Achieving Vividness; Ch. 27: Achieving Impressiveness.

Sarett, *Basic Principles of Speech,* Ch. 17: Oral Style.

Supplementary Reading in the Preaching Texts

Jones, *Principles and Practice of Preaching,* Ch. 10: The Style of the Sermon.

Oman, *Concerning the Ministry,* Ch. 12: Style and Speaking; Ch. 13: Style and Matter.

Writing Assignment

Discuss one of the following topics:
1. Characteristics of Good Speech Style
2. Methods of Improving Your Speech Style
3. Adapting Your Speech Style for the Pulpit
4. The Contribution of Style to the Total Speech Impact
5. Standards for "Correctness" in Style
6. Oral Style vs. Written Style

Speaking Assignment

Prepare and deliver a speech to fit the following requirements:

Subject: Any significant subject of your choosing. It must, however, be of more than local or individual significance. You have been able to fulfill previous assignments by talking about matters of little importance. For this speech, you should try to deal with an area of some scope and substance.

Method of organization: Any suitable plan. Be certain that the structure of your speech is appropriate for the subject matter, for your audience, and for the general purpose of the speech.

Purpose: To motivate in some manner.

Preparation: Involving the use of some research procedure. Research has not been required for your previous speeches; in fact, you were encouraged to speak from experience. This speech must extend beyond the limits of your personal experience at some point.

This speech is to be written out in full.

Delivery: To be read from manuscript.

Time: From 8 to 10 minutes. Since this is a manuscript speech, designed to give you experience in those situations where manuscripts are needed, the timing is an important factor. You should not speak for less than 8 minutes or for more than 10 (from 1,200 to 1,500 words).

Delivery will be from manuscript, but your audience should hear a speech, not an essay. Your manuscript should be written in an oral style, and you should be careful to maintain audience contact as you read.

Listening Assignment

1. In class, fill out a criticism sheet for each of the other speakers. Evaluate briefly: (a) the extent of the speaker's improvement as he has followed these assignments. Be specific. In what ways has the speaker improved? (b) the speaker's major shortcomings as a speaker. What, in your opinion, needs to be changed, and what would you suggest that he do about these needs?
2. Outside of class, listen to some speaker in a formal speech situation and write an analysis of his speech style. Did he express himself clearly, accurately, forcefully, correctly, and in a manner which was primarily oral rather than written? Try to note direct quotations from the speaker to illustrate and support your views.

12

Conclusion

You have finished your introduction to one of the most important areas in the modern curriculum. Rhetoric once ranked as a discipline basic to the entire educational structure. It declined during those periods of human history when tyranny oppressed the human spirit. It has risen to its central place once again with the development of democratic institutions and the growing importance of electronic aids to human communication. Few abilities will contribute as much to the impact which you are able to make on human society, whether for good or for ill, as your speech ability.

Unfortunately, the speech skills which any individual develops do not remain stable. Growing confidence and success may lead to lax habits of speech preparation. Little peculiarities of delivery may develop, individual quirks of which we are completely unconscious but which are extremely annoying to an audience. Mental laziness may lead to the development of what preachers call a "hobby"—some topic which so captures our interest that we discuss it every time we speak.

Insofar as speech is the product of our physical bodies, the sheer passage of time may cause our ability to deteriorate.

These changes are especially unfortunate in view of the fact that all of us have much room for improvement as speakers. Speech is a relatively deficient function. No man is as effective at oral communication as he would like to be or could be. Talented and hardworking as we are, we never achieve perfection in the invention of ideas, the arrangement of our thoughts, the development of our memories, the expression of ourselves in language, or our ability to deliver a speech.

If these considerations are true, you should regard your study of this text as merely the beginning of your efforts to develop yourself as a speaker. You have not arrived at a stopping point; you have merely passed a milestone in a long journey. Make plans immediately for moving ahead. Some of the following suggestions may help you:

1. *Gain all the experience you can.* Never miss an opportunity to speak. If you are an assistant pastor or a youth director, your pastor may be willing to let you supply the pulpit occasionally. Teach a Sunday school class. Volunteer for positions of community responsibility.

2. *Appoint a critic.* Ask some honest, frank individual (perhaps husband or wife) to note your irritating speech habits and call them to your attention. Any thoughtful, attentive individual will do; the critic need not be a professional. Speech problems which distract one listener probably disturb others also. Begin with the most obvious difficulty and eliminate it.

3. *Seek a variety of experience.* Speech includes many subordinate areas, and broadened experience in any one will contribute to your ability in the others. You may have an opportunity to speak on radio or before television cameras. If you are not preaching for the church service, you may be able to read the scripture. Perhaps you can join a community theater group for the acting experience.

4. *Join a speech-improvement group.* Your community prob-

ably has a Toastmasters Club. Membership will bring you further speech instruction, lots of experience, and some of the most direct and severe criticism you will ever receive. If you want to know what your hearers are really thinking, join Toastmasters and find out.

5. *Continue your formal study.* Even the repetition of a basic public speaking or speech fundamentals course would help to eliminate bad habits as they appear. Your local college or evening high school may also offer course work in drama, in radio and television, in oral interpretation, or in voice and diction. Advanced work in public speaking or in rhetorical criticism would also be helpful.

Whatever the extent of your talent as a speaker may be, develop it to the best of your ability. It can bring rich rewards, not only to you but to all who come in contact with you.

Appendix
Supplementary Reading Lists*

CHAPTER 1

In the Speech Texts

Baird, *Rhetoric: A Philosophical Inquiry,* Ch. 1: Boundaries and Applications; Ch. 2: Relationships to Categories of Learning; Ch. 5: Politics and Public Address.

Baker and Eubanks, *Speech in Personal and Public Affairs,* Ch. 1: First Thoughts About Speech Communication; Ch. 5: What Speech Is; Ch. 6: Speech as a Civilizing Force.

Brigance, *Speech: Its Techniques and Disciplines in a Free Society,* Ch. 1: The Rights of Listeners; Ch. 2: Four Fundamentals for Speakers.

Gray and Braden, *Public Speaking: Principles and Practice,* Ch. 1: Why Study Public Speaking; Ch. 4: Minimum Essentials for Good Speaking.

McBurney and Wrage, *The Art of Good Speech,* Ch. 1: The Role of Speech; Ch. 2: Standards of Good Speech; Ch. 3: Principles of Good Speech; Ch. 4: The Basic Course in Speech.

* For full publication information, see the bibliographies.

Oliver *et al., Communicative Speech,* Ch. 1: Oral Communication; Ch. 2: Standards of Effective Speech.

Ross, *Speech Communication: Fundamentals and Practice,* Ch. 1: Speech and Communication Processes.

Thonssen and Baird, *Speech Criticism,* Ch. 18: Toward a Philosophy of Rhetoric.

Weaver and Ness, *The Fundamentals and Forms of Speech,* Ch. 1: The Role of Speech in Contemporary Society; Ch. 2: The Nature of Communication and Speech.

In the Preaching Texts

Black, *The Mystery of Preaching,* Ch. 1: "Today Is Not Yesterday"; Ch. 2: A Preacher's Requisite.

Bowie, *Preaching,* Ch. 1: What Is Preaching? Ch. 2: The Man in the Pulpit, the Congregation, and the Message; Ch. 3: Three Aspects of the Preacher's Opportunity.

Broadus, *On the Preparation and Delivery of Sermons,* Introduction.

Brown, *The Art of Preaching,* Ch. 1: The Significance of the Sermon.

Buttrick, *Jesus Came Preaching,* Ch. 1: Is There Room for the Preacher To-day?

Garrison, *The Preacher and His Audience,* Ch. 1: A New Look at Preaching; Ch. 2: Motivation of Preacher and Listener; Ch. 3: The Communication of Meaning.

Kennedy, *His Word Through Preaching,* Ch. 1: We Are Ambassadors.

Luccock, *Communicating the Gospel,* Ch. 1: A Babel of Tongues.

Schloerb, *The Preaching Ministry Today,* Ch. 1: Ultimate Goals and Immediate Hazards.

Soper, *The Advocacy of the Gospel,* Ch. 1: The Situation of the Hearer; Ch. 2: The Preparation of the Preacher.

Thompson, *A Listener's Guide to Preaching,* Ch. 1: What Is Preaching? Ch. 4: Preparing for the Sermon.

Weatherspoon, *Sent Forth to Preach,* Ch. 3: The Nature of Preaching.

CHAPTER 2

In the Speech Texts

Baird and Knower, *General Speech,* Ch. 4: Finding Materials.

Baker and Eubanks, *Speech in Personal and Public Affairs,* Ch. 10: Producing Ideas: Thinking and Research.

Bryant and Wallace, *Fundamentals of Public Speaking,* Ch. 6: Collecting and Handling Information.

Capp, *How to Communicate Orally,* Ch. 6: How to Find, Record, and Analyze Your Material.

Dean, *Effective Communication,* Ch. 13: The Technique of Library Study.

Ehninger and Brockriede, *Decision by Debate,* Ch. 5: Obtaining Information: Printed Sources; Ch. 6: Recording and Filing Information.

Lomas and Richardson, *Speech: Idea and Delivery,* Ch. 3: Using New Ideas in Speeches.

McBurney and Wrage, *The Art of Good Speech,* Ch. 7: Exploring the Subject.

Monroe and Ehninger, *Principles and Types of Speech,* Ch. 9: Speech Materials: Sources, Records, and Classification.

Mudd and Sillers, *Speech: Content and Communication,* Ch. 7: Supporting Material: Sources.

Oliver *et al., Communicative Speech,* Ch. 5: Your Speech Materials.

Reid, *First Principles of Public Speaking,* Ch. 5: Gathering and Recording Material.

Sarett, *Basic Principles of Speech,* Ch. 7: Discovering Ideas: Sources and Methods.

Thonssen and Gilkinson, *Basic Training in Speech,* Ch. 15: Investigation.

In the Preaching Texts

Blackwood, *The Preparation of Sermons,* Ch. 7: The Call for Other Materials.

Bowie, *Preaching,* Ch. 4: Resources for Sermons.

Garrison, *Creative Imagination in Preaching,* Ch. 6: Five Ways to Increase the Value of Your Notes; Ch. 7: Scripture's Lens Changes All Seeing; Ch. 14: New Frontiers in Your Study.

Gibson, *Planned Preaching,* Ch. 8: Gathering and Storing Materials.

Koller, *Expository Preaching Without Notes,* Ch. 6: The Sources of Preaching Material; Ch. 18: The Systematic Filing of Materials.

Luccock, *In the Minister's Workshop,* Ch. 16: Collecting and Assimilating Material; Ch. 19: Making the Unconscious Mind an Ally; Ch. 20: To Toil Like a Miner Under a Landslide.

CHAPTER 3

In the Speech Texts

Baird and Knower, *General Speech,* Ch. 3: Choosing Your Subject and Purpose.

Brigance, *Speech: Its Techniques and Disciplines in a Free Society,* Ch. 3: First Steps in Managing Ideas.

Bryant and Wallace, *Fundamentals of Public Speaking,* Ch. 5: Selecting the Subject.

Capp, *How to Communicate Orally,* Ch. 5: How to Select Your Subject and Purpose.

Dean, *Effective Communication,* Ch. 2: The Purpose and the Audience.

Dickens, *Speech: Dynamic Communication,* Ch. 5: Speech Purposes.

Gray and Braden, *Public Speaking: Principles and Practice,* Ch. 13: Selecting a Speech Goal.

Hance *et al., Principles of Speaking,* Ch. 8: Selecting and Handling the Subject.

McBurney and Wrage, *The Art of Good Speech,* Ch. 5: Subjects for Speaking; Ch. 6: The Speaker's Purpose.

McCall and Cohen, *Fundamentals of Speech,* Ch. 3: Choosing Ideas.

Mudd and Sillars, *Speech: Content and Communication,* Ch. 3: Selecting a Subject.

Oliver and Cortright, *Effective Speech,* Ch. 8: Setting the Goal.

Oliver *et al., Communicative Speech,* Ch. 4: Purpose and Central Idea.

Reid, *First Principles of Public Speaking,* Ch. 4: Choosing Subject and Purpose.

Thonssen and Gilkinson, *Basic Training in Speech,* Ch. 14: The Ends of Public Speaking.

Weaver, *Speaking in Public,* Ch. 5: Subject and Purpose.

Wilson and Arnold, *Public Speaking as a Liberal Art,* Ch. 3: First Considerations.

In the Preaching Texts

Blackwood, *The Preparation of Sermons,* Ch. 3: The Beginnings of a Sermon; Ch. 8: The Choice of a Sermon Topic.

Broadus, *On the Preparation and Delivery of Sermons,* Ch. 3: The Subject.

Cleland, *Preaching to Be Understood,* Ch. 4: A Bow at a Venture?

Knott, *How to Prepare a Sermon,* Ch. 2: The Sermon Outline; Ch. 3: The Theme.

Whitesell and Perry, *Variety in Your Preaching,* Ch. 3: Vary the Subjects, Themes and Titles of Your Sermons; Ch. 5: Vary the Propositions, Key Words and Transitions of Your Sermons.

CHAPTER 4

In the Speech Texts

Baird and Knower, *General Speech,* Ch. 5: Organization and Outlining.

Baker and Eubanks, *Speech in Personal and Public Affairs,* Ch. 12: Planning the Introduction of Your Speech; Ch. 13: Planning the Body of Your Speech; Ch. 14: Planning the Conclusion of Your Speech.

Bryan, *Dynamic Speaking,* Ch. 4: Organizing and Outlining the Speech.

Bryant and Wallace, *Fundamentals of Public Speaking*, Ch. 9: Outlining the Informative Speech; Ch. 10: Introductions, Conclusions, and Transitions.

Capp, *How to Communicate Orally*, Ch. 8: How to Organize Your Speech.

Dean, *Effective Communication*, Ch. 7: Organizing and Developing Ideas.

Dickens, *Speech: Dynamic Communication*, Ch. 7: Speech Outlining; Ch. 8: Conclusions, Introductions, and Transitions.

Hance *et al., Principles of Speaking*, Ch. 10: Outlining for Speaking.

Lomas and Richardson, *Speech: Idea and Delivery*, Ch. 5: Organizing Speeches.

McBurney and Wrage, *The Art of Good Speech*, Ch. 12: The Organization of Speech.

McCall and Cohen, *Fundamentals of Speech*, Ch. 4: The Structure of Ideas.

Monroe and Ehninger, *Principles and Types of Speech*, Ch. 14: Selecting, Phrasing, and Arranging the Ideas Within the Speech; Ch. 15: Beginning and Ending the Speech.

Mudd and Sillars, *Speech: Content and Communication*, Ch. 4: Finding the Issues.

Oliver and Cortright, *Effective Speech*, Ch. 10: Organizing the Speech.

Oliver *et al., Communicative Speech*, Ch. 6: Organizing.

Phillips and Lamb, *Speech as Communication*, Ch. 6: Organizing Your Communication; Ch. 7: Outlining.

Reid, *First Principles of Public Speaking*, Ch. 8: Organizing: The Short Speech; Ch. 12: Beginning and Ending the Speech.

Thonssen and Gilkinson, *Basic Training in Speech*, Ch. 17: The Structure of Speeches.

Walter and Scott, *Thinking and Speaking*, Ch. 4: Organizing Ideas.

Weaver, *Speaking in Public*, Ch. 7: Structuring the Speech: Outlining.

Wilson and Arnold, *Public Speaking as a Liberal Art*, Ch. 8: Disposition: Organizing Materials; Ch. 9: Disposition: Outlining.

In the Preaching Texts

Davis, *Design for Preaching*, Ch. 11: Continuity: Introduction and Conclusion.

Ferris, *Go Tell the People*, Ch. 3: The Form of a Sermon I; Ch. 4: The Form of a Sermon II.

Garrison, *The Preacher and His Audience*, Ch. 7: Form and Order in the Skeleton of the Sermon.

Jordan, *You Can Preach*, Ch. 11: Introduction and Conclusion.

Luccock, *In the Minister's Workshop*, Ch. 12: Structure and Outline.

Oman, *Concerning the Ministry*, Ch. 20: Plan.

Phelps, *The Theory of Preaching*, Lectures 16 through 29, and 32 through 39.

Whitesell and Perry, *Variety in Your Preaching*, Ch. 8: Vary the Arrangement of Material in Your Sermon; Ch. 9: Vary the Conclusions of Your Sermons; Ch. 10: Vary Your Introductions.

CHAPTER 5

In the Speech Texts

Abernathy, *The Advocate*, Ch. 6: Audiences.

Baird and Knower, *General Speech*, Ch. 7: Adapting to the Audience and the Occasion.

Brembeck and Howell, *Persuasion*, Ch. 17; Finding the Available Means of Persuasion Within the Occasion and the Audience.

Capp, *How To Communicate Orally*, Ch. 4: How to Analyze the Audience and Speaking Occasion.

Clevenger, *Audience Analysis*, Chs. 1-7.

Dickens, *Speech: Dynamic Communication*, Ch. 12: Audience Analysis.

Gray and Braden, *Public Speaking: Principles and Practice*, Ch. 9: Analyzing the Audience.

Hance *et al.*, *Principles of Speaking*, Ch. 7: Understanding and Adapting to the Audience.

McBurney and Wrage, *The Art of Good Speech*, Ch. 11: The Audience and the Occasion: Analysis and Adaptation.

Monroe and Ehninger, *Principles and Types of Speech*, Ch. 8: Analyzing the Audience and the Occasion; Ch. 12: Selecting the Basic Appeal.

Mudd and Sillars, *Speech: Content and Communication*, Ch. 5: Analyzing the Audience.

Oliver and Cortright, *Effective Speech*, Ch. 11: Adapting to the Audience.

Phillips and Lamb, *Speech as Communication*, Ch. 5: Understanding the Listener.

Reid, *First Principles of Public Speaking*, Ch. 6: Adapting to the Audience.

Weaver, *Speaking in Public*, Ch. 3: The Listening Process; Ch. 4: The Occasion and the Audience; Ch. 17: Feedback.

White, *Practical Public Speaking*, Ch. 2: Analyzing the Specific Speech Situation.

Wilson and Arnold, *Public Speaking as a Liberal Art*, Ch. 4: Understanding Audiences.

In the Preaching Texts

Davis, *Design for Preaching*, Ch. 12: Tense and Mode.

Haselden, *The Urgency of Preaching*, Ch. 3: The Meaning of Relevant Preaching.

Jackson, *How to Preach to People's Needs,* Chs. 1-17.
Kennedy, *His Word Through Preaching,* Ch. 7: The Tension of Meeting.
Knox, *The Integrity of Preaching,* Ch. 5: Preaching Is Personal.
Luccock, *Communicating the Gospel,* Ch. 3: To Serve the Present Age.
Macpherson, *The Burden of the Lord,* Ch. 4: The Encounter.
Soper, *The Advocacy of the Gospel,* Ch. 3: The Arena of Preaching.
Stewart, *Heralds of God,* Ch. 1: The Preacher's World.

CHAPTER 6

In the Speech Texts

Baird and Knower, *General Speech,* Ch. 6: Developing Details; Ch. 13: Physical Activity and Visual Aids.
Baker and Eubanks, *Speech in Personal and Public Affairs,* Ch. 11: Kinds of Actualizing Detail.
Brigance, *Speech: Its Techniques and Disciplines in a Free Society,* Ch. 13: Supporting the Ideas.
Dickens, *Speech: Dynamic Communication,* Ch. 6: Speech Materials.
Gray and Braden, *Public Speaking: Principles and Practice,* Ch. 17: Weighing Facts and Arguments; Ch. 18: Visual Supports.
Hance *et al., Principles of Speaking,* Ch. 4: Materials of Development; Ch. 17: Audio-Visual Aids in Speaking.
Lomas and Richardson, *Speech: Idea and Delivery,* Ch. 4: Making Ideas Communicable.
McBurney and Wrage, *The Art of Good Speech,* Ch. 8: The Content of Speech; Ch. 9: Amplification.
McCall and Cohen, *Fundamentals of Speech,* Ch. 6: The Materials of Speech.
Monroe and Ehninger, *Principles and Types of Speech,* Ch. 10: Supporting the Main Points.
Mudd and Sillars, *Speech: Content and Communication,* Ch. 6: Supporting Material: Types and Uses; Ch. 15: Delivery: Visual Elements.
Oliver and Cortright, *Effective Speech,* Ch. 9: Selecting and Developing Ideas; Ch. 16: Using Visual Aids.
Oliver *et al., Communicative Speech,* Ch. 7: Developing Ideas; Ch. 11: Using Visual Aids.
Phillips and Lamb, *Speech as Communication,* Ch. 8: Supporting Ideas and Drawing Conclusions.
Ross, *Speech Communication: Fundamentals and Practice,* Ch. 8: Presenting Information.
Thonssen and Gilkinson, *Basic Training in Speech,* Ch. 18: Enforcement of Ideas: Forms of Discourse; Ch. 19: Enforcement of Ideas: Special Methods; Ch. 20; The Use of Visual Aids.
Walter and Scott, *Thinking and Speaking,* Ch. 3: Supporting Ideas.

In the Preaching Texts

Beecher, *Lectures on Preaching*—First Series, Lecture 7: Rhetorical Illustrations.

Blackwood, *The Preparation of Sermons,* Ch. 13: The Use of Illustrations.

Broadus, *On the Preparation and Delivery of Sermons,* Part III, Ch. 3: Illustration.

Davis, *Design for Preaching,* Ch. 14: Forms of Development.

Garrison, *The Preacher and His Audience,* Ch. 8: The Illustration: Putting Flesh on the Bones; Ch. 9: Humor in the Pulpit.

Jones, *Preaching and the Dramatic Arts,* Ch. 10: The Art of Using Story-Material.

Jones, *Principles and Practice of Preaching,* Ch. 8: Preparing Illustrative Material.

Jordan, *You Can Preach,* Ch. 15: Let Me Illustrate.

Macartney, *Preaching Without Notes,* Ch. 2: The Preacher and His Illustrations.

Oman, *Concerning the Ministry,* Ch. 21: Illustration.

Pattison, *The Making of the Sermon,* Ch. 17: Rhetorical Elements in the Sermon—Continued; Ch. 18: Rhetorical Elements in the Sermon—Continued.

Sangster, *The Craft of the Sermon,* Part II: Illustration.

Spurgeon, *Lectures to My Students* (The Art of Illustration), Lecture 1: Illustrations in Preaching; Lecture 3: The Uses of Anecdotes and Illustrations.

CHAPTER 7

In the Speech Texts

Baird and Knower, *General Speech,* Ch. 11: The Speaking Voice; Ch. 12: Articulation and Pronunciation.

Baker and Eubanks, *Speech in Personal and Public Affairs,* Ch. 17: Bodily Action; Ch. 18: Voice; Ch. 19: Articulation and Pronunciation.

Brigance, *Speech: Its Techniques and Disciplines in a Free Society,* Ch. 16: Being Seen; Ch. 17: Improving Voice Quality and Variety; Ch. 18; Being Heard and Understood.

Bryan, *Dynamic Speaking,* Ch. 13: Vocal Dynamics; Ch. 14: Dynamic Bodily Action.

Bryant and Wallace, *Fundamentals of Public Speaking,* Ch. 11: Intellectual and Communicative Aspects of Delivery; Ch. 12: Delivery: Methods of Development; Ch. 14: Voice and Pronunciation.

Dickens, *Speech: Dynamic Communication,* Ch. 9: Visual Communication; Ch. 10: Vocal Communication.

Fisher, *Improving Voice and Articulation,* Ch. 1: A Rationale for Speech Improvement; Ch. 2: Improving the Quality and Intensity of Phonation; Ch. 4: Variations in Rate, Loudness, and Pitch for Reinforcement of Meanings and Attitudes.

Gilman *et al., The Fundamentals of Speaking,* Ch. 7: Utterance: Voice, Articulation, Pronunciation; Ch. 8: Action: Poise and Physical Expression.

Gray and Braden, *Public Speaking: Principles and Practice,* Ch. 28: Vocal Aspects of Delivery; Ch. 29; Visible Aspects of Delivery.

McBurney and Wrage, *The Art of Good Speech,* Ch. 18: The Speaking Voice; Ch. 19: Use of the Voice in Speech; Ch. 20: Articulation and Pronunciation; Ch. 21: Bodily Action; Ch. 22: Delivery: Elements of Communication.

Monroe and Ehninger, *Principles and Types of Speech,* Ch. 4: Bodily Behavior on the Platform; Ch. 5: Improving Voice Quality; Ch. 6: Using the Voice: Communicating Ideas and Feelings.

Oliver and Cortright, *Effective Speech,* Ch. 13: Improving Bodily Expressiveness; Ch. 14: Improving the Voice; Ch. 15: Improving Articulation and Pronunciation.

Phillips and Lamb, *Speech as Communication,* Ch. 9: Delivery That Enhances the Spoken Word.

Reid, *First Principles of Public Speaking,* Ch. 13: The Body in Speech Making; Ch. 14: Improving the Speaking Voice; Ch. 15: Improving Articulation and Pronunciation.

Ross, *Speech Communication: Fundamentals and Practice,* Ch. 5: Bodily Action; Ch. 6: Voice and Articulation.

Sandford and Yeager, *Principles of Effective Speaking,* Ch. 5: How to Be Effective in the Way You Talk.

St. Onge, *Creative Speech,* Ch. 21: The Auditory Scenery; Ch. 22: The Visual Scenery.

Thonssen and Gilkinson, *Basic Training in Speech,* Ch. 6: Visible Symbols of Speech; Ch. 7: Audible Symbols of Speech; Ch. 10: The Sounds of English Speech; Ch. 11: Pronunciation.

Weaver and Ness, *The Fundamentals and Forms of Speech,* Ch. 6: The Visible Code; Ch. 7: The Audible Code.

Weaver and Ness, *An Introduction to Public Speaking,* Ch. 11: Developing Effective Visible Action; Ch. 12: Making the Voice Work.

Weaver, *Speaking in Public,* Ch. 11: Pronunciation and Diction; Ch. 13: The Science of the Voice; Ch. 14: The Story of the Voice; Ch. 15: The Tone of the Voice; Ch. 16: The Visual Story.

Wilson and Arnold, *Public Speaking as a Liberal Art,* Ch. 11: Delivery.

In the Preaching Texts

Bowie, *Preaching,* Ch. 11: Delivering the Sermon.

Garrison, *The Preacher and His Audience,* Ch. 11: Visual Elements in Preaching.

Kennedy, *His Word Through Preaching,* Ch. 4: If the Trumpet Sounds Indistinct.

Luccock, *In the Minister's Workshop,* Ch. 18: "Oft When the Word Is on Me to Deliver."

CHAPTER 8

In the Speech Texts

Baird, *Rhetoric: A Philosophical Inquiry,* Ch. 9: Structure.

Blankenship and Wilhoit, *Selected Readings in Public Speaking,* Ch. 3: Organization: The Arrangement of Ideas.

Borden, *Public Speaking—As Listeners Like It!,* Ch. 1: Listeners' Laws for Speech Organization.

Bryant and Wallace, *Fundamentals of Public Speaking,* Ch. 23: Speech Plans.

Gilman *et al., The Fundamentals of Speaking,* Ch. 4: Adaptation: Audience and Plans.

Hovland *et al., Communication and Persuasion,* Ch. 4: Organization of Persuasive Arguments.

McBurney and Wrage, *The Art of Good Speech,* Ch. 13: The Methods of Inquiry.

Mills, *Message Preparation: Analysis and Structure,* Ch. 5: Outlining and Patterns of Arrangement.

Wilson and Arnold, *Public Speaking as a Liberal Art,* Ch. 8: Disposition: Organizing Materials; Ch. 9: Disposition: Outlining.

In the Preaching Texts

Blackwood, *The Preparation of Sermons,* Ch. 12: The Variety of Sermon Plans.

Bowie, *Preaching,* Ch. 9: Constructing the Sermon.

Jones, *Principles and Practice of Preaching,* Ch. 6: Outlining the Sermon: Types of Outlines.

Jordan, *You Can Preach!* Ch. 21: Blueprints.

Sangster, *The Craft of the Sermon,* Part I, Ch. 3: Sermons Classified According to Structural Type.

CHAPTER 9

In the Speech Texts

Abernathy, *The Advocate,* Ch. 8: Ethical Persuasion.

Baird and Knower, *General Speech,* Ch. 8: Developing Confidence; Ch. 14: The Speaker's Personality.

Baker and Eubanks, *Speech in Personal and Public Affairs,* Ch. 2: Developing Poise and Self-Confidence.

Brembeck and Howell, *Persuasion,* Ch. 13: Finding the Available Means of Persuasion Within the Speaker.

Buehler and Linkugel, *Speech: A First Course,* Ch. 1: Poise and Confidence; Ch. 2: The Speaker's Image.

Hovland *et al., Communication and Persuasion,* Ch. 2: Credibility of the Communicator.

Oliver and Cortright, *Effective Speech,* Ch. 2: How to Speak Communicatively; Ch. 3: The Personality of the Speaker.

Ross, *Speech Communication: Fundamentals and Practice,* Ch. 2: Emotion and Confidence.

Sarett, *Basic Principles of Speech,* Ch. 3: The Person Who Speaks.

Thonssen and Baird, *Speech Criticism,* Ch. 13: The Character of the Speaker.

Thonssen and Gilkinson, *Basic Training in Speech,* Ch. 4: Social Adjustment; Ch. 5: Personality.

Walter, *Speaking to Inform and Persuade,* Ch. 8: The Ethos of the Speaker.

White, *Practical Public Speaking,* Ch. 1: Approaching Public Speaking Positively.

In the Preaching Texts

Bartlett, *The Audacity of Preaching,* Ch. 1: The Claim: Incredible but Inescapable.

Beecher, *Lectures on Preaching* (First Series), Lecture 3: The Personal Element in Oratory.

Brown, *The Art of Preaching,* Ch. 8: The Soul of the Sermon.

Gibson, *Planned Preaching,* Ch. 7: The Preacher Himself.

Haselden, *The Urgency of Preaching,* Ch. 4: Recovering the Preacher's Identity.

Jarvis, *If Any Man Minister,* Ch. 5: The Preacher as Man.

Jones, *Principles and Practice of Preaching,* Ch. 3: The Preacher's Part in His Preaching.

Luccock, *In the Minister's Workshop,* Ch. 2: The Minister Himself.

MacLennan, *Pastoral Preaching,* Ch. 5: The Pastor Preaching.

Phillips, *Bearing Witness to the Truth,* Ch. 5: The Preacher and the Truth.

Scherer, *For We Have This Treasure,* Ch. 2: Like a Man of God.

Simpson, *Lectures on Preaching,* Ch. 3: The Preacher Personally.

Stewart, *Heralds of God,* Ch. 5: The Preacher's Inner Life.

CHAPTER 10

In the Speech Texts

Baird, *Rhetoric: A Philosophical Inquiry,* Ch. 4: Logic and Reason in Discourse; Ch. 7: Emotional Response.

Baird and Knower, *General Speech,* Ch. 17: Argumentative Speaking; Ch. 18: Persuasive Speaking.

Bettinghaus, *Message Preparation: The Nature of Proof,* Ch. 5: Logical Proof: Inference; Ch. 6: Motivational Proof: Judgments; Ch. 7: Strategy and Tactics in Message Preparation.

Brembeck and Howell, *Persuasion,* Ch. 6: The Social Basis of Persuasion; Ch. 8: Reasoned Discourse in Persuasion.

Brigance, *Speech: Its Techniques and Disciplines in a Free Society,* Ch. 7: The Architecture of Persuasion; Ch. 24: Dynamic Persuasion in an Industrial Democracy.

Bryant and Wallace, *Fundamentals of Public Speaking,* Ch. 18: The Audience: Motives and Basic Lines of Thought; Ch. 20: Suggestion; Ch. 21: Proposition, Evidence, and Logical Support.

Corbett, *Classical Rhetoric for the Modern Student,* Ch. 2: Discovery of Arguments.

Dean, *Effective Communication,* Ch. 15: Rational Persuasion—I; Ch. 16: Rational Persuasion—II; Ch. 17: Irrational Persuasion.

Dickens, *Speech: Dynamic Communication,* Ch. 16: Building Audience Attitudes; Ch. 17: Releasing Audience Attitudes.

Ehninger and Brockriede, *Decision by Debate,* Ch. 8: The Unit of Proof and Its Structure; Ch. 9: Evidence; Ch. 13: The Nature and Sources of Belief.

Freeley, *Argumentation and Debate,* Ch. 8: Reasoning; Ch. 9: The Structure of Reasoning; Ch. 19: The Role of Motivation.

Gilman *et al., The Fundamentals of Speaking,* Ch. 3: Exposition and Persuasion: Forms and Principles.

Gray and Braden, *Public Speaking: Principles and Practice,* Ch. 10: Using Motive Appeals; Ch. 11: Attention and Interest; Ch. 17: Weighing Facts and Arguments.

Hovland *et al., Communication and Persuasion,* Ch. 3: Fear-Arousing Appeals.

Monroe and Ehninger, *Principles and Types of Speech,* Ch. 13: Choosing Material That Will Hold Attention; Ch. 22: The Speech to Convince.

Mudd and Sillars, *Speech: Content and Communication,* Ch. 9: Attention and Interest; Ch. 10: Argument: Logical Elements; Ch. 11: Argument: Psychological Elements.

Napiecinski and Ruechelle, *Beginning Speech,* Unit IV: Persuasion and Intellectual Appeals; Unit V: Persuasion and Psychological Appeals.

Oliver and Cortright, *Effective Speech,* Ch. 19: The Speech to Induce Belief; Ch. 20: The Speech to Move to Action.

Reid, *First Principles of Public Speaking,* Ch. 17: Persuading Through Argument; Ch. 18: Persuading Through Emotions, Attitudes.

Ross, *Speech Communication: Fundamentals and Practice,* Ch. 9: The

Psychology of Persuasion; Ch. 10: The Logical Supports of Persuasion.

Sarett, *Basic Principles of Speech,* Ch. 12: Managing Ideas: Argumentation.

Weaver and Ness, *An Introduction to Public Speaking,* Ch. 9: Holding the Attention of an Audience; Ch. 10: Motivating an Audience.

Weaver, *Speaking in Public,* Ch. 10: Logical Integrity.

In the Preaching Texts

Broadus, *On the Preparation and Delivery of Sermons,* Part III, chapter 2: Argument.

Jones, *Preaching and the Dramatic Arts,* Ch. 6: The Psychology of Influencing Character.

Pattison, *The Making of the Sermon,* Ch. 15: Rhetorical Elements in the Sermon—Continued; Ch. 16: Rhetorical Elements in the Sermon—Continued.

Sangster, *The Craft of the Sermon,* Part I, Ch. 4: Sermons Classified According to Psychological Method.

Soper, *The Advocacy of the Gospel,* Ch. 5: Evangelistic Preaching.

CHAPTER 11

In the Speech Texts

Abernathy, *The Advocate,* Ch. 10: Verbalization—Semantic Aspects.

Baird, *Rhetoric: A Philosophical Inquiry,* Ch. 8: Language and Style.

Baird and Knower, *General Speech,* Ch. 9: Using Effective Language; Ch. 10: Language and Semantics.

Baker and Eubanks, *Speech in Personal and Public Affairs,* Ch. 16: Language in Speech.

Beardsley, *Thinking Straight,* Ch. 2: Some Verbal Pitfalls; Ch. 3: Levels of Meaning; Ch. 4: Figurative Language.

Brembeck and Howell, *Persuasion,* Ch. 9: The Language of Persuasion; Ch. 20: Composing the Persuasive Speech.

Brigance, *Speech: Its Techniques and Disciplines in a Free Society,* Ch. 15: Using Words.

Bryant and Wallace, *Fundamentals of Public Speaking,* Ch. 16: The Language of the Speech.

Buehler and Linkugel, *Speech: A First Course,* Ch. 10: Language in Life; Ch. 11: Language in the Speech.

Capp, *How to Communicate Orally,* Ch. 11: How to Use Language Accurately and Effectively.

Corbett, *Classical Rhetoric for the Modern Student,* Ch. 4: Style.

Dickens, *Speech: Dynamic Communication,* Ch. 11: Verbal Communication.

Gilman *et al.*, *The Fundamentals of Speaking*, Ch. 5: Communication: Thought, Language, and Style.

Hance *et al.*, *Principles of Speaking*, Ch. 11: Style in Speaking.

Lomas and Richardson, *Speech: Idea and Delivery*, Ch. 7: Style: Ideas and Language.

McBurney and Wrage, *The Art of Good Speech*, Ch. 17: Language and Style.

McCall and Cohen, *Fundamentals of Speech*, Ch. 7: Language.

Monroe and Ehninger, *Principles and Types of Speech*, Ch. 18: Wording the Speech.

Mudd and Sillars, *Speech: Content and Communication*, Ch. 12: Language and Oral Style.

Oliver and Cortright, *Effective Speech*, Ch. 12: Improving the Style of Your Speech.

Oliver *et al.*, *Communicative Speech*, Ch. 8: Attention, Interest, and Style.

Phillips and Lamb, *Speech as Communication*, Ch. 10: The Language of Communication.

Reid, *First Principles of Public Speaking*, Ch. 16: Improving Your Use of Words.

Ross, *Speech Communication: Fundamentals and Practice*, Ch. 3: Language: Meaning and Use.

Thonssen and Baird, *Speech Criticism*, Ch. 15: The Style of Public Address.

Weaver and Ness, *The Fundamentals and Forms of Speech*, Ch. 8: The Language Code; Ch. 9: Meaning.

Weaver and Ness, *An Introduction to Public Speaking*, Ch. 13: Making Language Work.

Weaver, *Speaking in Public*, Ch. 12: The Speech and Rhetoric.

White, *Practical Public Speaking*, Ch. 14: Using Language in Delivering the Speech.

Wilson and Arnold, *Public Speaking as a Liberal Art*, Ch. 10: Style.

In the Preaching Texts

Blackwood, *The Preparation of Sermons,* Ch. 16: The Marks of Effective Style.

Broadus, *On the Preparation and Delivery of Sermons*, Part IV: The Style of the Sermon.

Davis, *Design for Preaching*, Ch. 15: Writing for the Ear.

Davis, *Principles of Preaching*, Ch. 12: Style.

Garrison, *The Preacher and His Audience*, Ch. 5: Problems and Opportunities of Style.

Jordan, *You Can Preach!* Ch. 8: The Language of the Sermon.

Koller, *Expository Preaching Without Notes*, Ch. 17: The Minister's Vocabulary.

Luccock, *In the Minister's Workshop,* Ch. 17: Words Are the Soul's Ambassadors.
Sangster, *Power in Preaching,* Ch. 4: Make It Plain.
Scherer, *For We Have This Treasure,* Ch. 6: The Way You Handle the Word of Truth.

Bibliographies of Books Assigned

Bibliography of Speech Books and General Works

Abernathy, Elton. *The Advocate.* New York: David McKay Co., 1964.

Adler, Mortimer J. *How to Read a Book.* New York: Simon & Schuster, 1940.

Anderson, Virgil A. *Training the Speaking Voice.* 2nd ed. New York: Oxford University Press, 1961.

Aristotle. *The Rhetoric.* (*Great Books of the Western World,* ed. Robert Maynard Hutchins, Vol. IX.) Chicago: Encyclopaedia Britannica, 1952.

————. *The Rhetoric of Aristotle.* Trans. by Richard Claverhouse Jebb. Cambridge: Cambridge University Press, 1909.

Baird, A. Craig. *Rhetoric: A Philosophical Inquiry.* New York: The Ronald Press Company, 1965.

Baird, A. Craig, and Knower, Franklin H. *General Speech.* 3rd ed. New York: McGraw-Hill Book Company, 1963.

Baker, Virgil L., and Eubanks, Ralph T. *Speech in Personal and Public Affairs.* New York: David McKay Co., 1965.

Beardsley, Monroe C. *Thinking Straight.* Englewood Cliffs, N. J.: Prentice-Hall, 1950.

Bettinghaus, Erwin P. *Message Preparation: The Nature of Proof.* Indianapolis: The Bobbs-Merrill Co., 1966.

Blankenship, Jane, and Wilhoit, Robert. *Selected Readings in Public Speaking.* Belmont, Calif.: Dickenson Pub. Co., 1966.

Borden, Richard C. *Public Speaking—As Listeners Like It!* New York: Harper & Row, 1935.

Brembeck, Winston L., and Howell, William S. *Persuasion.* Englewood Cliffs, N. J.: Prentice-Hall, 1952.

Brigance, William N. *Speech: Its Techniques and Disciplines in a Free Society.* 2nd ed. New York: Appleton-Century-Crofts, 1961.

Bryan, Martin. *Dynamic Speaking.* New York: The Macmillan Company, 1962.

Bryant, Donald C., and Wallace, Karl R. *Fundamentals of Public Speaking.* New York: Appleton-Century-Crofts, 1960.

Buehler, E. C., and Linkugel, Wil A. *Speech: A First Course.* New York: Harper & Row, 1962.

Capp, Glenn R. *How to Communicate Orally.* Englewood Cliffs, N. J.: Prentice-Hall, 1961.

Clevenger, Theodore, Jr. *Audience Analysis.* Indianapolis: The Bobbs-Merrill Co., 1966.

Corbett, Edward P. J. *Classical Rhetoric for the Modern Student.* New York: Oxford University Press, 1965.

Dean, Howard H. *Effective Communication.* Englewood Cliffs, N. J.: Prentice-Hall, 1953.

Dickens, Milton. *Speech: Dynamic Communication.* 2nd ed. New York: Harcourt, Brace & World, 1963.

Ehninger, Douglas, and Brockriede, Wayne. *Decision by Debate.* New York: Dodd, Mead & Co., 1963.

Fisher, Hilda B. *Improving Voice and Articulation.* Boston: Houghton Mifflin Company, 1966.

Freeley, Austin J. *Argumentation and Debate.* 2nd ed. Belmont, Calif.: Wadsworth Publishing Co., 1966.

Gilman, Wilbur E., *et al. The Fundamentals of Speaking.* 2nd ed. New York: The Macmillan Company, 1964.

Gray, Giles Wilkeson, and Braden, Waldo W. *Public Speaking: Principles and Practice.* 2nd ed. New York: Harper & Row, 1963.

Hance, Kenneth G., *et al. Principles of Speaking.* Belmont, Calif.: Wadsworth Publishing Co., 1962.

Hovland, Carl I., *et al. Communication and Persuasion.* New Haven: Yale University Press, 1953.

Hutchins, Robert Maynard, ed. *The Great Ideas: A Syntopicon II.* (*Great Books of the Western World,* Vol. III.) Chicago: Encyclopaedia Britannica, 1952.

Lomas, Charles W., and Richardson, Ralph. *Speech: Idea and Delivery.* Boston: Houghton Mifflin Company, 1956.

McBurney, James H., and Wrage, Ernest J. *The Art of Good Speech.* Englewood Cliffs, N. J.: Prentice-Hall, 1953.

McCall, Roy C., and Cohen, Herman. *Fundamentals of Speech*. 2nd ed. New York: The Macmillan Company, 1963.

Mills, Glen E. *Message Preparation: Analysis and Structure*. Indianapolis: The Bobbs-Merrill Co., 1966.

Monroe, Alan H., and Ehninger, Douglas. *Principles and Types of Speech*. 6th ed., Glenview, Ill.: Scott, Foresman & Company, 1967.

Mudd, Charles S., and Sillars, Malcolm O. *Speech: Content and Communication*. San Francisco: Chandler Publishing Co., 1962.

Napiecinski, Thomas H., and Ruechelle, Randall C. *Beginning Speech*. Boston: Allyn and Bacon, 1964.

Oliver, Robert T., and Cortright, Rupert L. *Effective Speech*. 4th ed. New York: Holt, Rinehart & Winston, 1961.

Oliver, Robert, *et al. Communicative Speech*. 3rd ed. New York: Holt, Rinehart & Winston, 1962.

Phillips, David C., and Lamb, Jack Hall. *Speech as Communication*. Boston: Allyn and Bacon, 1966.

Reid, Loren. *First Principles of Public Speaking*. 2nd ed. Columbia, Mo.: Artcraft Press, 1962.

Ross, Raymond S. *Speech Communication: Fundamentals and Practice*. Englewood Cliffs, N. J.: Prentice-Hall, 1965.

Sandford, William, and Yeager, Willard. *Principles of Effective Speaking*. 6th ed. New York: The Ronald Press Company, 1963.

Sarett, Alma Johnson, ed. *Basic Principles of Speech*. 4th ed. Boston: Houghton Mifflin Company, 1966.

St. Onge, Keith R. *Creative Speech*. Belmont, Calif.: Wadsworth Publishing Co., 1964.

Thonssen, Lester, and Baird, A. Craig. *Speech Criticism*. New York: The Ronald Press Company, 1948.

Thonssen, Lester, and Gilkinson, Howard. *Basic Training in Speech*. 2nd ed. Boston: D. C. Heath & Company, 1953.

Walter, Otis M. *Speaking to Inform and Persuade*. New York: The Macmillan Company, 1966.

Walter, Otis M., and Scott, Robert L. *Thinking and Speaking*. New York: The Macmillan Company, 1962.

Weaver, Andrew T., and Ness, Ordean G. *The Fundamentals and Forms of Speech*. Rev. ed. New York: The Odyssey Press, 1963.

Weaver, Andrew T., and Ness, Ordean G. *An Introduction to Public Speaking*. New York: The Odyssey Press, 1961.

Weaver, Carl H. *Speaking in Public*. New York: American Book Company, 1966.

White, Eugene E. *Practical Public Speaking*. 2nd ed. New York: The Macmillan Company, 1964.

Wilson, John F., and Arnold, Carroll C. *Public Speaking as a Liberal Art*. Boston: Allyn and Bacon, 1964.

Bibliography of Homiletics Books

Bartlett, Gene E. *The Audacity of Preaching*. New York: Harper & Row, 1962.

Beecher, Henry W. *Lectures on Preaching* (First Series). New York: Fords, Howard and Hulbert, 1881.

Black, James. *The Mystery of Preaching*. Westwood, N. J.: Fleming H. Revell Company, 1924.

Blackwood, Andrew W. *The Preparation of Sermons*. Nashville: Abingdon Press, 1948.

Bowie, Walter R. *Preaching*. Nashville: Abingdon Press, 1954.

Broadus, John A. *On the Preparation and Delivery of Sermons*. Rev. by John Weatherspoon. New York: Harper & Brothers, 1944.

Brooks, Phillips. *Lectures on Preaching*. New York: E. P. Dutton & Co., 1877.

Brown, Charles. *The Art of Preaching*. New York: The Macmillan Company, 1922.

Bryan, Dawson C. *The Art of Illustrating Sermons*. Nashville: Abingdon-Cokesbury Press, 1942.

Buttrick, George A. *Jesus Came Preaching*. New York: Charles Scribner's Sons, 1931.

Cleland, James T. *Preaching to Be Understood*. Nashville: Abingdon Press, 1965.

Davis, Henry G. *Design for Preaching*. Philadelphia: Muhlenberg Press, 1958.

Davis, Ozora S. *Principles of Preaching*. Chicago: University of Chicago Press, 1924.

Farmer, Herbert. *The Servant of the Word*. New York: Charles Scribner's Sons, 1942.

Ferris, Theodore. *Go Tell the People*. New York: Charles Scribner's Sons, 1951.

Forsyth, P. T. *Positive Preaching and Modern Mind*. London: Hodder & Stoughton, 1907.

Garrison, Webb B. *Creative Imagination in Preaching*. Nashville: Abingdon: Press, 1960.

————. *The Preacher and His Audience*. Westwood, N. J.: Fleming H. Revell Company, 1954.

Gibson, George M. *Planned Preaching*. Philadelphia: The Westminster Press, 1954.

Haselden, Kyle. *The Urgency of Preaching*. New York: Harper & Row, 1963.

Jackson, Edgar N. *How to Preach to People's Needs*. Nashville: Abingdon Press, 1956.

Jarvis, E. D. *If Any Man Minister*. London: Hodder & Stoughton, 1951.

Jeffs, H. *The Art of Sermon Illustration*. 2nd ed. Westwood, N. J.: Fleming H. Revell Company, n.d.

Jones, E. Winston. *Preaching and the Dramatic Arts.* New York: The Macmillan Company, 1948.

Jones, Ilion T. *Principles and Practice of Preaching.* Nashville: Abingdon Press, 1956.

Jordan, G. Ray. *You Can Preach!* Westwood, N. J.: Fleming H. Revell Company, 1951.

Kennedy, Gerald. *His Word Through Preaching.* New York: Harper & Brothers, 1947.

Knott, H. E. *How to Prepare a Sermon.* Cincinnati, Ohio: The Standard Press, 1927.

Knox, John. *The Integrity of Preaching.* Nashville: Abingdon Press, 1957.

Koller, Charles W. *Expository Preaching Without Notes.* Grand Rapids, Mich.: Baker Book House, 1962.

Luccock, Halford E. *Communicating the Gospel.* New York: Harper & Brothers, 1954.

————. *In the Minister's Workshop.* Apex ed. Nashville: Abingdon Press, 1944.

Macartney, Clarence E. *Preaching Without Notes.* Nashville: Abingdon Press, 1946.

MacLennan, David A. *Pastoral Preaching.* Philadelphia: The Westminster Press, 1955.

Macpherson, Ian. *The Burden of the Lord.* Nashville: Abingdon Press, 1955.

Oman, John. *Concerning the Ministry.* New York: Harper & Brothers, 1937.

Pattison, T. Harwood. *The Making of the Sermon.* Rev. ed. Philadelphia: The American Baptist Publication Society, 1941.

Phelps, Austin. *The Theory of Preaching.* New York: Charles Scribner's Sons, 1893.

Phillips, Harold C. *Bearing Witness to the Truth.* Nashville: Abingdon-Cokesbury Press, 1949.

Sangster, W. E. *The Craft of the Sermon.* London: The Epworth Press, 1954.

————. *Power in Preaching.* Nashville: Abingdon Press, 1958.

Scherer, Paul. *For We Have This Treasure.* New York: Harper & Row, 1944.

Schloerb, Rolland W. *The Preaching Ministry Today.* New York: Harper & Brothers, 1946.

Simpson, Matthew. *Lectures on Preaching.* New York: Nelson and Phillips, 1879.

Soper, Donald. *The Advocacy of the Gospel.* Nashville: Abingdon Press, 1961.

Spurgeon, C. H. "The Art of Illustration" in *Lectures to My Students.* Grand Rapids, Mich.: Zondervan Publishing House, 1955.

Stewart, James S. *Heralds of God*. New York: Charles Scribner's Sons, 1946.

Thompson, William D. *A Listener's Guide to Preaching*. Nashville: Abingdon Press, 1966.

Weatherspoon, Jesse B. *Sent Forth to Preach*. New York: Harper & Brothers, 1954.

Whitesell, Faris D., and Perry, Lloyd M. *Variety in Your Preaching*. Westwood, N. J.: Fleming H. Revell Company, 1954.

INDEX

221

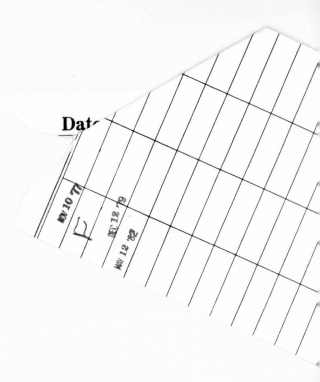

Date

NOV 10 77

DEC 18 '79

MAY 12 '82